The Dude Circus

The Dude Circus

Grab your popcorn for my funny and freakish stories of online dating as a midlife ticket holder

Rose Heyze

RINGMASTER PRESS
Columbus, OH

Ringmaster Press

Columbus, Ohio

Library of Congress Control Number: 2023905759

Paperback ISBN: 979-8-218-17479-8

eBook ISBN: 979-8-218-17480-4

Book cover design by Danae Pickens

Interior design by Christina Thiele

Editorial production by kn literary

www.thedudecircus.com

To every single person looking for love on the internet. And to my running friends—I couldn't have made it without you.

Contents

Built to amaze, built to astonish—but age still matters.

Don't blame a clown for acting like a clown. Ask yourself
why you keep going to the circus.

One monkey off your back, but the circus is still in town.

Peep show, anyone?

It's the greatest show on Earth! Stay for a while.

Even the most entertaining show comes to an end.

Introduction

I reentered the dating world during the first months of the COVID pandemic, right after my marriage of twenty-two years ended. Dating for the first time since 1995 seemed exciting—initially. Since my only dating experience harkened back to a time when cell phones and the internet didn't exist, I had no idea what I was about to embark upon. My sister had dated online for decades with only recent success. But somehow, with zero modern dating experience myself, I thought it would be easy. What did I know? Well. Nothing, it turns out. This humbling experience led me down a road of insanity. The logical action would have been to halt in my tracks and step off the path. But what I encountered was hard to pivot away from as it also provided humor and entertainment. It was one of the most shocking and eye-opening experiences of my life—both in good and uncomfortable ways. There were times I took a pause to reevaluate if it was something that was worth the effort and emotional energy. But I came back to feeling that the hope of finding love outweighed how crazy looking for it was, and I would jump right back in.

I'm confident, attractive, own my own businesses, have friends, am extroverted, have high self-esteem, know that I look younger than my age, and felt I had the chutzpah to meet someone this way. I figured my assets would allow for a quick and easy dating stint. Weren't all my characteristics what men my age were looking for in a partner? Seemed like it would be a cake walk. I'd put my cutest pictures on my profile, say what I was looking for, and *boom*, Prince Charming would jump out of the phone and into my life. But I discovered that just because I know I'm a great catch, doesn't mean men were looking for the catch I provided.

As the months went by, and the world of online dating exposed its increasingly bizarre side, I realized that writing about my experiences helped me "dump" all the stories from my head; if I wrote about what was happening, I could keep my emotions in check. It was a way for my brain to stay sane in an insane world. If I didn't journal about the crazy, I would go crazy. Once I started journaling, my expectations and hopes changed, I realized there were rules to the system that I hadn't learned yet, and I found out that if I just went in expecting the worst but hoping for the best, I wouldn't feel crushed when things didn't work out.

Today's dating subculture, with its focus on technology, is the craziest experience you will ever embark upon. I'm sharing my experiences to help you navigate this dude circus, to remember that you are amazing, and to realize that one day someone else will see that too. While I was lucky to share the ups and downs of the ride with my closest girlfriends, they still didn't know how it felt on the inside. They could laugh and be shocked at the stories I told them, but then they went home to the comfort of their husbands. The feelings of rejection and disrespect that happen because of men you barely know can only be felt by my fellow online-dating comrades. Those of you who have entered the Fourth Dimension trying to find "your person" understand the conflicting thoughts of staying in the game, wondering if the Matrix will ever spit out someone who's worth it. For me, it was a strange "pull" to stay for the show, to see what would happen next, to hang on to the thin tightrope of hope that I might catch a winner. I needed to laugh at the bizarre stories and insane behavior and work hard to not personalize men's responses—or lack thereof. Online dating isn't for sissies or for the faint of heart. This shit will step on your feelings, stomp on your spirit, and smother your soul if you let it. But if you stay in and laugh and write about it, you may just find your purpose in this journey.

I have a silly wooden sign on my deck that says, "Welcome to the Dick Circus." It was an impulsive Etsy purchase. Having raised two young men, divorced a man, supervised men, and had friends who are men, it made me laugh to imagine them as a circus. The parallels make me shake my head and smile—entertaining and silly, sometimes shocking, surprising, and daring—and I felt like the humorous part needed a visual reminder, hence the sign. During my dating months, when I stepped outside in the mornings with my coffee, seeking nature and solitude, I'd see the sign and remember to always laugh when things felt hard. The concept of a circus fits my experience with dating in the very best ways. The circus is entertaining, hysterical, freakish, difficult to watch sometimes, but you keep going back. It's hard to turn away, and the shock value of the acts pulls your eyes toward the show. The circus has hardworking, mindful, diligent tight-rope walkers and silly, scary clowns who run around squeezing their noses. We don't want to attend daily, but when given the opportunity, purchasing a cheap ticket gets us some great thrills and some exciting times.

I thought hard about what I was looking for when I dove into the ring. I wanted something in the middle: I didn't need to find my next husband, but I also wasn't interested in one-night stands. I wanted something monogamous and real, but it didn't have to get serious. What unfolded was a tightrope act—a precarious balance between serious and casual that wasn't easy to find. While there was a thrill to the performance and finding the balance, men didn't seem to understand what the middle meant.

As if that weren't enough, who knew how hard it would be to meet someone in what I found to be a totally backward way? Asking questions for days to be sure you're a "match" isn't how it's done in the face-to-face world. When you meet someone at a bar, at work, or at the grocery store, you "feel" the chemistry and connection first. You ask questions about politics and religion later.

When you date online, you ask all the questions first to find that perfect someone on screen, only to meet them and not feel the feelings. Or you feel them, but they don't. It's funny. You'd think that on date one, you would know if you both felt good about things. But there is this strange fear of the unknown and whether he's going to "change his mind," even if everything was amazing. For whatever reason, that fear isn't there when you meet someone the old-fashioned way. Maybe because online dating demands you "pick" someone based on a few comments and a picture, while meeting naturally—in person at a park or bar, say—you "feel" the connection first. But you learn early on, at least I did, that no matter how good that first online connection feels, it can disappear in the blink of an eye. And all that work up front seems like so much energy to keep spending. The thing is, we keep going in because of our innate craving for love, for interaction, and for the chemical release that comes with the high of a new relationship.

The following chapters will give you stories of my online dating experience, what I learned as I jumped into this unknown world, and the lessons that helped me stay sane and laugh a lot along the way. Some chapters will teach you the rules I learned, some will help you decide for yourself what rules you need to develop, some will give you my personal experiences and feelings, and, hopefully, all of them will teach you lessons you can take with you along your own journey. Maybe a few stories will even make you laugh out loud or shake your head, a grin on your face. As I processed the stories of the men out loud with my friends, it helped me realize that putting everything in print could create an authentic and genuine dating guidebook. If I, as a therapist with decades of experience in human behavior can get hurt over and over again, laugh about it, then move on with new resolve and new rules, then maybe all of us together can find a way through dating with more excitement and humor and less frustration and pain.

Welcome to the circus. Enjoy the show.

Despair is the clown's
constant companion.

CHAPTER 1

Is Everyone Broken?

On February 13, 2019, I slipped on a hidden patch of ice while running with my friends. I shattered my ankle and broke my tibia.

I had been a distance runner for nearly ten years, and run through many winters with careful confidence. My friends and I knew when to avoid the roads and when to skip the run altogether. We prided ourselves on how we navigated these decisions and often laughed at folks who ran in unadvisable conditions, calling them careless and stupid. Despite being careful, mindful, and diligent, I fell anyway. In my defense, we all saw the ice and announced, "Let's move to the grass. There's ice here." But as I moved to the grass, I stepped on snow that had a sheet of ice underneath. I put my foot down, and my ankle started to roll. I threw myself backward, held my arms up, and fell the way we all learned to fall, protecting my wrists. It was a harbinger of things to come: that need for constant protection as I "fell" through the dating world.

Christie, my Girl Scout bestie, wanted to splint my ankle with sticks and a jacket and get me in a car. "Nope, call an ambulance," I said as I stared down at my right knee pointing left and my right foot pointing right. I believe my exact words were, "I'm fucked." A year of four surgeries, a slow-to-heal tibia, and seven months in a boot ensued.

My broken leg became a metaphor for what happened in my life in the days, weeks, and months that followed. During my recovery, I dwelled on problems in my marriage I had ignored for years, and I learned I was stronger than I ever knew. I learned I had some of the most loyal and dedicated friends anyone could hope for as they surrounded me with everything I needed. I learned that laugher cures almost anything and how you look at a situation determines how you feel. As a therapist, I knew all of this in theory. But when you become your own client, you learn things through difficult practice.

Before my fall, I walked the earth with confidence—and I didn't walk slowly. I did things I needed to do and wanted to do, and I felt like I had it made. I taught classes, trained groups, did therapy, went out with friends, ran, did yoga, and hustled through my days. Then I fell, and I had to sit, think, rest, and evaluate my life. Was it what I wanted? My mortality flashed before my eyes, and I realized that my life was at least half over. A close inspection into what was supposed to be my closest intimate relationship with my partner showed that it wasn't healthy.

I hadn't fully understood my marriage was broken. Not in every way. If it had been broken to pieces like my ankle, I would have done something years ago. No, my marriage was broken in insidious ways. My husband didn't want to work on a list of issues that I wanted to address, including more time connecting, less drinking, and less time focused on himself. I no longer wanted to be in a marriage where he would do "his thing" on weekend mornings, drink alcohol the rest of the afternoon, and then expect me to be the designated driver on our way out for dinner. These date nights that started with a drunk, self-involved husband had become his way to tell everyone we had wonderful, connected time together, keeping up the masquerade that things were good. Lack of sex and intimacy, unless you counted a quickie every once in a while, was part of our normal. The biggest issue that was screaming in my face was how self-focused my husband truly was. The day in the hospital after my emergency ankle surgery—with corrective metal rods on the outside of the ankle for two weeks to allow the skin to heal before more surgery—I looked straight into the eyes of the man I had been married to since 1998 and said, "You have to pick up the slack now."

His reply? "I don't think I can."

Telling me he couldn't be counted on was the beginning of my understanding of what was lacking in our marriage.

I asked him to seek a therapist (I already had one) to work on things we had overlooked for years. We are both therapists, so this request seemed logical to me. Easy and appropriate. We had been married almost twenty-two years. There were decades to fight for, and things could be fixed. Right?

Well, things can only be fixed if a person thinks they need fixing. My husband refused to get help, stating he could help himself. And I knew that putting the puzzle pieces back together without his work and self-reflection would be nearly impossible. Broken isn't one-sided. And as I requested and was denied, I discovered that breaking my ankle allowed me to realize I had a right to fight for what I wanted. My life was a series of active and moving to-do lists. I never really stopped until I slept, so this injury forced introspection—sitting still and thinking about the decades of time spent together, about the things I had "let go" because I figured it was just what happened to marriages. I had taken on most of the parenting while still working full time. I had to "ask" my husband to "help" with the kids so I could get more accomplished for the house. I ran in the early mornings before anyone woke up so I could still be around for the kids even if their father was home. There was no lying, cheating, or stealing. But there was also no partnership. I wanted a *partner*, and I wanted my partner to be healthy and our relationship to be solid and meaningful.

While my ankle got fixed, my marriage stayed unfixed, and as the year turned, I decided that ending it was the only option. It was a tough decision. I had married someone outside my religion, which had been very difficult for my parents. My family is very close, and as the older daughter and the first one to find a serious relationship, everyone had ideas on what kind of guy I should marry. The one I picked had qualities and characteristics that seemed worth fighting for, so I convinced my parents they could trust me. I fought for my family's support all those years. With this story in my mind—and frustration and sadness in my heart—I took a deep breath, knowing that, despite a few great years, many good years, and then a handful of very difficult ones, it was time to turn a corner.

With a ton of support, a healing ankle, and my wits intact, I stated what I wanted: a divorce. I knew it wasn't going to be easy, but nothing worth doing is easy. I learned through my fall and working with clients over the years that sometimes big decisions need to be made to create the life we need and want. A famous Helen Keller quote I keep in my office was part of my inspiration to keep moving forward: "When one door of happiness closes, another opens; but often we look so long at the closed door that we do not see the one which has been opened for us." I hoped that allowing myself to close the door on my marriage would open new doors I didn't even know existed.

This was in February of 2020, and we all know what was already in motion: a worldwide health pandemic. My ankle was broken, my marriage was broken, and now the world seemed to be breaking. And while this may seem like doom and gloom and truly apocalyptic, it was all a strange and necessary part in my story. When I was able to begin my running career again, I also began a new journey: dating online. Of course a new relationship couldn't fix my heart from the loss of a broken marriage, but I was hopeful that the excitement of dating again would be a fun and playful way of moving forward. It was the beginning of many things, and I had high hopes that repair was on its way.

But plot twists kept coming, and my story led me to the brokenness of online dating, and these new experiences were not what I expected. I'd thought I'd hop on my phone and meet a great guy. Easy. Relatively early, it became clear that I wasn't the only person to have left a broken marriage. What that meant for the connections and the interactions was eye-opening and challenging. I learned that most men didn't take the interactions seriously—at least at first. Many of them treated me like this was all "pretend" or a game, and

I quickly understood that this term *broken* extended to the hearts of the guys on the other end of the phone.

The first sign that this new dating world was going to be something I wasn't prepared for was when, planning to meet for a walk outside, a guy asked, "Where are we going to have sex?" COVID times had led to carefully planned outdoor meetings, and this guy's first concern was how and when we were going to have sex? And that's when I thought, *Wow, here we are! This guy's wondering where we'll have sex, but he won't even let me in his house because of possible contagion.* Irony plagued these months of dating: men would risk their lives for sex—but only if it was outside.

One of my first steady dudes (we made it a couple of months) was a broken US marine named Sam. (Aren't many men who have experienced combat often broken?) Well, this one had brooding depression written all over him, but he was also adorable, sexy, sweet—and the worst communicator ever. We had a marathon first date that started with lunch, then visiting his dogs at his house, followed by dinner at my house. We laughed together, joking about how the date was lasting so long that by the time we were having dinner, it felt like a second date. He seemed real and kind, and we loved the same music. The chemistry was fierce, despite the seventeen-year age difference, and it appeared, at first, to be the perfect middle.

But like the circus, things aren't always as they seem. Sam went days without texting, only to suck me right back in by sending me one of his depressing poems in the middle of the night. He kept talking and texting just enough to keep me coming back. He was kind and loving and missed his kids. His ex-wife had cheated with his best friend, then asked for an open relationship, and eventually moved six hours away with their kids. Sam was left in a two-bedroom condo with his dogs. He was working on his bachelor's degree, was in the reserves every other weekend, and seemed to want something real when we were together.

This one was rough. He was the first dude who grabbed at my heart and made me wonder if, after only a couple of months of online dating, I could have possibly found someone to invest my heart in. I had real feelings for him.

I came to realize that I feel a strange comfort in connecting with the broken male. I like to fix and help and make things better for people. Sam was a good man who couldn't take how good I was being to him. He couldn't grasp that some women aren't disloyal, and he hadn't healed from what had happened to him. Sam seemed to be still in love with his ex-wife and couldn't get a handle on connecting in a healthy way with me.

So why was he on the app in the first place? Welcome to the lonely, broken man. They want someone and then they can't follow through. They think the app is the place for a fresh start, but when they're faced with a real woman with a real life, they aren't healthy enough to begin again.

At first, I thought Sam was the one who got away, but as time went on, I realized I was destined for more. While he had potential, his kind of broken was the kind I worked on fixing as a therapist, not as a partner. I didn't have to find projects to mend. With the understanding that everyone is struggling to some degree, I pressed on, knowing that broken comes in all sizes, and this guy was big-time broken.

———

As a therapist, I like to look at things through a positive filter, rather than being disappointed with a situation that seems very negative and upsetting upon initial inspection. I often attempt to fix my feelings with humor. But when it came to my experiences with broken men, what came to mind was a necklace a close friend gave me after I broke my leg. The necklace had a stone disk that had been "repaired" with broken streaks of gold and was accompanied by a kintsugi poem.

Kintsugi, which translates as "golden joinery," is a gorgeous Japanese practice also known as *kintsukuroi*, meaning "golden repair." It is the Japanese art of repairing broken pottery by mending broken areas with a lacquer that is dusted or mixed with gold, silver, or platinum. The philosophy behind the practice is to treat the breakage, or broken part, along with the repair as an integral part of the history of the object instead of something to hide.

Once I thought of brokenness as being integral to a beautiful and meaningful story, I stopped worrying about covering the scars on my ankle with vitamin E, and I was willing to see them as my warrior wounds. The theme of brokenness continued to play in my mind. And as I jumped online to see what online dating was about, it occurred to me that everyone is broken in some way. Maybe embracing the cracks in our lives is the way to go. Accepting that there is meaning behind them is important, and it was perhaps my way of embracing the online dating madness and thinking of it as a true circus.

While the theme of brokenness may have sad and depressing undertones, it did help set the stage for what my expectations needed to be and how my coping skills needed to grow.

Not my circus, not my monkeys,
and don't count your chickens.

The New Rules

The rules of online dating aren't posted anywhere obvious. There may be books on what women should consider when they start dating on an online platform, but I didn't consult any. Not because I was overconfident. I honestly believe I was simply naive. It's embarrassing to admit now, but it had never occurred to me I would need instructions before diving into the circus ring. And what a ring it was. Beasts and clowns everywhere you look.

I quickly learned how wrong I was as the rules revealed themselves to me in time and without warning. Sometimes I learned the hard way; others (gratefully), I learned by accident before I met the dude. I found that online dating was a new full-time job, and as the manager I needed to embrace the madness as I learned the rules of the system.

Early on, I discovered one of the first rules is that the possibility of a relationship often hinges on texting. You need to text just the right amount: not too much to look needy but not too little to look uninterested. Navigating this felt like a texting tightrope: imagine being twenty-five feet above ground without a net, flailing your arms and hoping the person who catches you when you fall is one of the good ones. It took gigawatts of emotional energy.

As I navigated the new dating world that clearly needed some good fixing, I realized there was a learning curve. It was tough to catch on to, and at first, I was hanging on by my fingernails. But as the weeks and months went by, I started to learn how to navigate it.

The first lesson learned was that I needed to insist on either a phone call or a FaceTime call before agreeing to meet in person. I figured this out after one of the earliest dates I set up turned into a bust. Thomas the Tattoo Guy and I had been texting for about five days before planning a date. Later in my dating journey, as I became more experienced, I would have seen the red flags: He wanted to meet at a bar, but I insisted we meet at a familiar place near me. In the thirty minutes leading up to the date, he texted delay after delay and excuse after excuse. As I sat at the bar, waiting for him, he texted that he had been pulled over by a cop and was getting a ticket. I realized I was being stood up, and I was so confused by the huge games. Just tell me you're not coming, dude. He had played the lie for a long time, and when I thought to look him up on social media (in my defense, I only knew his first name), I saw the "In a Relationship" status immediately.

So, no more just texting. A phone or FaceTime call was better than a text to get an idea of if there was any chemistry between us. Tone and volume were there, and the way a conversation would flow, or not, was more apparent. I could gauge their seriousness about meeting for a date by their willingness to share their voice me.

Remaining somewhat anonymous at first was important as well. One evening I was telling a friend over dinner that I was sure all the dating men in Columbus knew that I had broken my leg, had gotten divorced, and run long-distance. I had found myself telling the elevator pitch of who I was so many times I got tired of hearing about myself. But many of the guys didn't know the name of my business or even my last name. It came intuitively to not give out any identifying information. I figured out early on that safety came first, as I would talk to these men and realize I had no idea if they were telling the truth at all. Anyone can say anything. My best friend's husband is a police officer, and she told me to share my location with her whenever I decided to go to a guy's home. With her concerns and advice in my mind, more and more rules began to develop.

With safety in mind, I also decided that a big operating

rule of mine would be to always go to the same restaurant for first dates. I became very friendly with the servers at a place near my house, and they deserve a huge shout-out for being there for me through those months. They always made it clear to any date that they knew me, they asked me how things had gone when I was back in for dinner with friends, and they consoled me if I got stood up. The manager came up with the idea that if I ever felt unsafe at any time during a date, I would ask for the "special wing sauce." It would be my code to indicate that I felt uncomfortable or in trouble, and the staff could intervene, or one of them could walk me to my car if I wanted to leave a date quickly. Even without my asking for the special wing sauce, they had my back. "Rose, you good? You need anything?"

The staff there also protected my spirit. Laughing with the servers and bartenders saved me on many occasions, and as they became part of my safety team, they also became part of my humor team, helping me move forward to the next date. Although I never had to order the special sauce, I felt braver knowing it was ready for me at any time.

During the first weeks I was online, I was texting with what appeared to be a dream guy. He told me he was a widower and that talking about his kid was off limits. I really liked that he was protective about his son. He messaged all the right things, focusing on how he was looking for a kind, fun, working go-getter, and loved women who are independent and sure of themselves. He asked about me and appeared interested. I gave him my phone number, knowing I could always block him. I had already learned that quickly switching from the dating app to the phone made sense. But it was also useful to see if guys would abuse the privilege and start sending dirty pictures or ask for them from me. The dating app I used didn't allow pictures during the message exchange, so I wanted to weed out the dirt balls before expending too much emotional energy. This guy seemed legit, and as the days went by, he texted good morning, responded quickly, and seemed sweet. But sometimes if something seems too good to be true, it's exactly that.

At one point, he texted about how he loved pink flowers. I mentioned this to my running pal, and she said, "Rose! This guy isn't real."

"Huh? What do you mean? He's texting me. You think he's a robot or an alien?"

She told me that the pink flowers were a tell for a catfish: a guy who is eventually going to ask for money. She explained that she and a friend (they were also both dating online), had been in contact with a guy who seemed amazing and then talked about pink flowers. They realized they were talking to the same guy. We decided that it was very likely this was the same guy since all our stories were so similar. She noted that maybe my guy was a real guy, and the pink flowers was just a coincidence, but that seemed unlikely.

That night, I asked him to FaceTime with me, and he disappeared. Just vanished into thin air as quickly as he had materialized. That's when I realized that online dating was also a place for trolls, and the place needed to be patrolled. Reporting these dudes became a part of my mission. There was a place on the app to report them and explain your reasons. I hoped by doing so, I could perhaps save another woman from a suspicious guy. I was, after all, a helping professional, and if I could save the dating women of the world from slippery suckers, I was totally going to do it. Adding rules to the dating playbook was now my job. The rule I added to my list here was to be very careful if someone seemed too good to be true. I would ask for that FaceTime call earlier on, and I would report anyone who stopped talking to me after I requested that call.

After my pink-flowered faker, I noticed a trend. The fake dudes always had generic names, were "new to the site," and looked too young for their "in their forties" age claims. Their targets were middle-aged women since they assumed we're desperate. Well, this desperate woman wasn't *that* desperate. As my cousin and friend Nikki said, "You're barking up the wrong tree, bitch!" When I think of this saying, I see an invincible tree standing tall with a lot of other trees supporting it. These fakers were the freak-show part of the circus that needed to be stopped. So I kept reporting them in hopes of slowing them down.

———

My pal Kevin, who is also making his way through the online dating world, is the inspiration for another rule of this journey. Despite our many differences—he's a single, twenty-nine-year-old male; I'm a divorced woman in her late forties—we would laugh, joke, share heartbreak stories, compare the number of frustrating scenarios we'd encountered over a week, and analyze the train wrecks that we both seemed unable to turn away from.

Kevin is one of my anchors, and I'm not sure he even knows the role he played in helping me build the armor I needed to protect my self-esteem. He and I have been transparent with our friendship and what we mean to each other. We use the word *love* when we describe our platonic bond, but I'm not sure he really understands that he was on the top of my list to call when things went sideways with a date. He always knew what to say. Perhaps it's because he, too, is a trained therapist? Maybe even more than that—he has been in the circus too and knows the dangers. And when you know, you know. These knowing conversations helped to develop my rules, as each conversation turned from empathizing with my pain to creating a rule to attempt to avoid the same kind of pain next time.

He always reminded me how amazing I am and how young I look. "Rose, you know how this goes: no expectations and don't count your chickens before they hatch." Because even when I had a great first date, and the date said how great it was, most of the time they were gone by the next day. It happened to him too, and we talked about the lack of communication and the way folks come and go without warning. He told me his stories of feeling disappointed and exhausted by the emotional commitment of texting for days without things working out.

So "no chickens" became our tag line when we liked someone: "The date went so well; we have another one set up for tonight! But *no chickens*!" It was a rule to help avoid getting attached to someone too early, and it helped to create an emotional armor against disappointment. "Well, he's gone, but since I knew it could happen, I'm okay with it." Protecting myself against getting excited about the possibility of a relationship was sad in a way, as I really couldn't feel that feeling without waiting for a significant amount of time to pass. This resulted in what I now call *online dating trauma*, where you have a really hard time trusting any guy who's said he likes you.

This is how Kevin and I protected our egos and our souls. We'd remind each other of our worth, and we'd move on. Like fast. Always keeping in mind my friend Christie's wise words: "Rose, there is always another one." And you know what? Christie is always right.

So, despite my desire to date only one guy at a time, some bowed out so quickly I begrudgingly decided to allow myself to talk to a few at the same time. This next rule allows you to talk to a few guys at once, even if your morals and values demand you only get serious with one at a time. After a couple of dates, simply make your decision on who you connect with more. Doing this allowed me to feel more in control and not as disappointed when one fell through for one reason or another. I made the rules during the pandemic, so dating more than one dude seemed kind of gross—and dangerous. But I knew the guys did it, so I told myself I would talk to as many as I could keep track of simultaneously (inserting special nicknames for them on my contact list) but wouldn't date more than two, and wouldn't sleep with more than one at a time.

And off I went into the world of my new job. Managing my dating app became the hustle on my list of real-job hustles that I didn't get paid for. And really, I rarely even got a meal out of it. The current cultural rule of dating seems to be that splitting the check is the norm, and someone paying for your meal is rare. *Sigh.* At the very least, give me a nice, good free dinner with your side of stupid. I decided that if someone paid on the first date, the old-fashioned gesture meant something. But alas, it wasn't often the case. When the guy did pay, well, he made it through a hoop many did not. It wasn't a required hoop, though; the rule to only date a guy again if he did pay didn't make the list. But in my mind, it meant they were certainly interested in at least doing something very nice. And very nice is a good thing.

What followed from dating more than one guy at once was the rule to keep track of whom I was talking to and allow myself to have fun with the list. *Wait, did I tell this one about my broken leg? Does this one know I have kids? Does this one know I'm an addictions specialist? Shit, I forget.*

I went on a girl's weekend with a friend, and I had nine guys in the queue. So she and I made flashcards for them: age, job, how nice they were, if they texted back, if I had met them in person yet. Then we ordered the cards on a table by how much I was digging them at the time. By the time the next weekend rolled around, the queue had changed. Seriously! Even after twenty-four hours the queue could change. It was an emotionally exhausting game, but it was also ridiculous and funny—and the best material a distance-running girl could bring to the table.

When the girls and I would go on a run, they would save me for last. "Okay, Rose, it's your turn. What's the queue looking like?"

"It's looking like a bunch of men not following through, ladies. Per usual. But I'm still here, front row and center to the shit show, and for whatever reason, I continue to play the ringmaster."

Was it because I was hopeful things would turn around? Honestly, I'm not sure. I found myself getting so upset when I'd invest and lose, reinvest and lose, take a chance and lose, that I would delete the app, only to go back on relatively quickly. I'm either a glutton for punishment or a hopeful romantic. Or both? Definitely both.

One of the most interesting rules I learned early on was about profile pictures. You need to post pictures that really look like you, and it should include at least one that shows your whole body. Of course, folks strategically pick pictures to highlight their good points. And men seem to want full-length pictures so they can see your size. Early on, I just posted head shots, because they were the prettiest ones I had. When I'd start talking to a guy, he'd ask for more pictures. At first, this really upset me. How chauvinistic and judgmental could they be? Chris, older than me by about four years, came up to the bar where I was waiting for him for our first date and said, "Thank God! The last girl I met looked like she ate her pictures."

I was so upset, mostly because he actually said it out loud to me. I understand not being attracted to a woman who is heavier than she looks in her picture, but he didn't have to say that!

I used to think men were the shallowest of all when they asked for more pictures—dirty pictures, sexy pictures, foot pictures, heels pictures, leg pictures. Then I went on a date with a man whose picture didn't match reality. We had been texting and talking on the phone for a week. He was close to my age, witty, had a great job, was ready to date but not looking for a wife, and also wanted something more than casual sex. I was so attracted to his pictures I became cautiously excited as the days went by. My running girls and I wondered if maybe this could be the real deal.

As I was driving to the restaurant for our first date, I saw a man with a mask pulled tightly around his very large, round face. He started waving at me, and I realized he was my date. He was about 100 pounds heavier than his pictures—and that is when I started to understand the rule. It hit me at once: accurate, full-length pictures do indeed matter! Did he think

I wouldn't notice?

I'd like to think that I'm not shallow, but when someone deliberately withholds information about their looks by posting old photos, what else could they be holding back? I was more upset that this guy withheld information from me, thinking it was okay. A heavy guy wasn't a deal breaker for me, but a liar was.

I learned to always tell someone exactly what I expected, that talking dirty too fast by text was one of my deal breakers, and if they asked me for any picture that didn't include my clothing, I was out. The rules helped me weed out men, and truthfully, juggling a long queue of possibilities just wasn't realistic and fun anyway.

I realized that the rules men seem to make can be a difficult learning curve, but my rules helped me navigate the turns. This juggling act showed me that if you aren't completely good at your craft, something will fall. At least creating some of my own rules helped me feel like a part of the show and not just a constant casualty. And while I hated that this had become a game, I realized that playing it was part of finding the "one." I can play too, boys, and I know how to do it: have my own rules, stick by them, and stay strong. Ironically, as soon as I got good at the rules, I was able to leave the game. And with the right rules and a little bit of luck, you will be able to leave too.

Dating is a circus, and I'm stuck in
the freak tent.

CHAPTER 3

The Creepy Shit

How would I define *creepy?* It's tough. Some of the things I'm about to tell you might not seem creepy if your boyfriend or husband were saying them to you. If you're in a relationship, and you're being silly, having fun, playing around, maybe some dirty talk or some pics can be fun, welcome, and totally edgy and thrilling. But when you're trying to meet a man, and your profile clearly states, "No one-night stands; looking for someone who actually wants to date, someone who is serious about finding a partner; and looking for good communication, trust, and honesty," you'd think you'd get men who are like-minded—men who want to meet you and see if this could be real. But not this girl. I appear to attract anyone and everyone—or maybe they're just looking for sex? I look at my pictures and my words, and I think to myself, *Did I ask for weird shit?* Nope. But here I was, in a world of totally different morals, values, and ideas on boundaries than when I exited the dating scene in 1996.

And wow. It was something to behold. Perhaps all this creeper stuff has always been around, but online dating just amplifies it? When someone can hide behind a screen, showing only what they want to show through pictures and the written word, it seems to allow bolder and bigger behaviors. Some guys would give identifying information to the point of telling me where they worked. This would give me false hope, thinking that anyone who was so forthcoming and honest wouldn't have a creepy side. But I guess everyone has a different sense of what *creepy* means, and these guys could certainly use a lesson on what type of words hook women. Or maybe they didn't want a lesson, and just threw out the same hook so many times, they figured they'd catch something eventually. I'm embarrassed to admit that I sometimes accepted the bait. It certainly made for some good stories, that's for sure.

So let's talk creepy. Creepy is relative right? Creepy can slither into the conversation in many different forms. I like to define creepy by how it makes me feel: The goosebumps that come in a bad way, sliding up your arms and making you squirm in your chair. That feeling in your gut that screams to your intuition to stop and turn back! So many different comments can make the creepy creep up your body: sexist, racist, misogynistic, fetishistic, being too sexual too soon, to name a few. I mean, I feel like I'm somewhat sexually free and open for a late forties, recently divorced girl from the eighties, when no one I knew came out as gay, and porn was a dirty magazine your friend's dad had hidden beneath the bed. Am I too prudish or scared? Am I open? Am I free spirited? Maybe all of it? All I can say is the offers I got were strange and far reaching—from total strangers! Is this the way things really were? Should I just go with it and let 'er ride? Or did a one-liner like "Message me; I hope you appreciate *huge*," mean I should run for the hills? "Huge" could be good right? But when your opening line before you meet me is "Message me; I'm *huge*," that's bad right?

And so it went. One-liners arrived in a steady stream, never leaving me wanting for more.

Would you be willing to wear a remote-controlled sex toy between your legs when we go to dinner, with high heels on, with the remote in my hand?

I'm at a bible study. I'll get back to you soon, but just know, I'm really a dirty boy. I actually like it when you're mean to me.

I'm going to send you my hard dick under a blanket, so you can see the size but not SEE it!"

I'm actually in a relationship with someone now, and I'm a heroin addict, but I was hoping I could go on a date with you to test out whether or not still I want to be with my girlfriend.

Will you sit on my face and ride me, my queen? I'm craving you. Please!

Can I get a picture of you in high heels and nothing else?

Can I get a picture of your feet? I have a foot fetish.

Can we have phone sex now?

I wanted to know where we would have sex if we decide to meet? There is a pandemic, so you can't come to my house.

Have you ever considered having a submissive rub your feet, wash your clothes, and clean your house?

I won't lie—that last one made me pause for a second. But . . . no! These creepy one-line, introductory messages were so unbelievable I had to make a conscious decision to laugh. When the comments were sexual in nature, instead of deleting the guy off my phone immediately, I actually found myself egging them on a bit to get them going. I would get right in there and allow them to talk more specifically about what they wanted to do to me and with me. I'd use their language and ask questions to elicit more detail. I decided that I needed to take control of what was happening instead of feeling nauseous and grossed out. I figured if I played along, I wouldn't feel so uncomfortable. I began to realize that these exchanges were even more amusing if I shared them, so I started telling my girlfriends about them during our morning runs to save my sanity. Was I even still sane? All these thoughts ran through my head: *Maybe this is the way dating works now, and I just need to get used to it. Maybe I'm just a prude, and I need to toughen up. Maybe this guy could be cool in person. Do I give him a chance? If I rule out* all *the creep factors, I'm literally left with a few stragglers, and those guys seem boring. Do I push through, or do I delete?*

They were tough calls. Because, really? Part of me liked the creep show. I believe most of us have a part that is so intensely curious about what makes people behave this way that sometimes it is hard not to encourage it. Like a train wreck. Who can turn away? Even if we should.

As my dating goals changed, my decisions to delete these responses came quicker and quicker. At first, I really thought I could find "the middle." I didn't need a serious relationship after twenty-two years of marriage, but I didn't want a one-night stand either. Asking men for "something in the middle" —monogamous but not necessarily serious—seemed like an open invitation for the guys to get super dirty with the conversation. If you tell a guy "I don't need something serious," they immediately go to the extreme and think, *She must want casual sex.* When I explained that no, I do not want casual sex, I'd like a real connection, dates, something monogamous, they'd go to the other extreme and think, *Oh, she wants to get married.* Trying to explain that I wanted something in the middle never got easier. So, what I asked for kept morphing and changing to attract the "right dudes." As soon as I decided to go ahead and advertise for something "real" and possibly serious, the creepers came with less force, and the ability to "delete the creep" that did squeeze through my barriers was easier.

But then, one day, I got the following, immediately after we matched. *Matching* means I liked his profile or he liked mine, and then we liked each other back, and we could now talk privately on the app. After three or four exchanges, I got this request "Would you be willing to have sex with another man while I watch? If not, it's a deal breaker."

A deal breaker? I have to *want* to have sex with *other men while you watch*? What in the actual holy hell happened to this guy as a child? *Okay, no, dude!* But the therapist in me got curious, and I asked him where this was all coming from. He insisted that he meant it as *empowering* for a woman, so she would feel like she could just do anything. And this from a dude whose profile picture included his young daughter. This is also where my vocabulary grew, and my knowledge of the truly creepy expanded. He called it *hotwifing*. And apparently it's a real thing. But not for me. Nope, not for me.

Creepy can't be highlighted any better than when I dated a racist by accident. Oh boy, did I have to process that one. I'm not sure where my head was with all the warning signs—because upon reflection, there were many. The first should have been when he showed up at the restaurant early so I couldn't see that he was anti-mask—something I found out only later. Other signs were he couldn't stand his parents, lived in a tiny studio, and hated his new job. But he could kiss for three hours straight and was skilled at it too. He was extremely sexy and attractive and seemed to be very interested in *me* as much as in how I looked. He was cute, and I guess I was in a vulnerable place. I can't be superwoman with a badass self-image all the time, can I? Well, this is where I learned that I needed to be always on point, on task, careful, mindful, and listening to my intuition, not ignoring it because *this can be just fun and casual, so it doesn't matter if he's not everything I need.*

He told me he was a survivalist and sent me pictures of

him camping alone with no gear, just some tools and a sleeping bag. He mentioned a program where he learned to survive in the wilderness and proudly described his skills in great detail. He was in his thirties, had never been married, had no kids, so I mistakenly figured, the less baggage, the less bother. Shit. I was dead wrong.

He had no relationship history because a relationship with this guy would mean a man-is-the-boss dynamic. My liberal self started to open her eyes to the red flags only after I had decided that going camping with him was a good idea. I can't believe I put myself alone in the woods with him. I'm either an idiot or I was in some skewed delusion that this could work. Lesson learned. If someone isn't like you in all the important ways, stop, look, and listen. Your gut is powerful and your intuition strong. Trust them and yourself before you try to fit a square peg into a round hole. The peg won't fit.

When we were in the car on our way to camping, the guy announced that he was a racist. He literally said, "Rose, have I told you I'm a racist?" *Wait. Did he just say racist? Even racists don't say it out loud!*

All I could think about was my bestie with her Black husband and biracial kid, and I just wanted to roll him out of the car. Instead, I spent twenty-eight hours with this fuck show. I guess I felt stuck and thought that if I asked to leave, it would trigger his anger.

He cut down a tree for firewood, which is illegal. I just sat there hoping with all my might that no one would notice as he chopped the poor, tall tree into tiny pieces that didn't even burn well. Remember how he told me he went to survival school? Well, get this: It was a freezing cold March day, and he showed up for camping in jeans, no underwear, no extra blankets, a sleeping bag with no hood, no winter coat, no gear, no food, no cooking supplies, no lights, no lighter, and no gloves. As we hiked, he talked about wanting a woman who would just "do what I say." I asked, "Like in the Middle Ages?" And he said, "Oh yes, that would be ideal." *Ideal?* He mentioned that he listened to some radio talk show that leans super conservative. *OMG, I'm gonna die!*

Although I never really felt in imminent danger, I also knew that his creepiness factor was strong. My job was to lay low, stay cool, sip my beer, and keep things chill. I would not talk about my liberal self, my fear of right-wing thinking, or how stupid he was. Nope. *Shhhhhh.*

And if this shit couldn't get weirder, it did. He told me in quiet confidence that he had a sex doll. I'm talking about a life-size-woman kind of fake girlfriend he could fuck-and-fold kind of toy. Fuck in "all the ways" kind of toy. He asked my opinion. "Does that bother you, Rose?" I carefully and quickly considered how to respond. My therapy skills are strong, and as I looked him dead in the eyes, I knew my reaction was important here. *I am in the woods, in the dark, not leaving until the morning.* My mental answer to him was, *Um, not at all, you racist, misogynistic fuck-show of an excuse for a man.* But to his face I said, "Not at all," with as little expression on my face and emotion in my soul as I could muster. He said the toy cost him $800 and that he kept her in the closet. Gulp. But alas, I was stuck in a tent with him for the night, so I made it through, then dropped him quickly. And it was after this debacle that I decided vaccinated, masked, and left-leaning dudes were my only dudes. Even if it was just for fun.

———

Remember that you get to decide what creepy means to you. I realized that when I decided to have fun with the dirty talk, it made me feel more in control of the situation. I learned that I could handle creepy in the sexual sense, but not when it came with a dose of racism or misogyny. I decided who I would delete because things were feeling wrong and who I would entertain because things were feeling playful. I learned that talking about my experiences to my friends kept things amusing. The side-splitting laughter that came from this storytelling kept me going back in for more if the situation allowed. So creepy is creepy if it's creepy to you. You get to decide, with a little help from your friends, the definition that speaks to your soul. But remember, if your skin crawls and your gut speaks, trust yourself. Because if it looks like a duck and acts like a duck, it's a fucking creepy-ass duck!

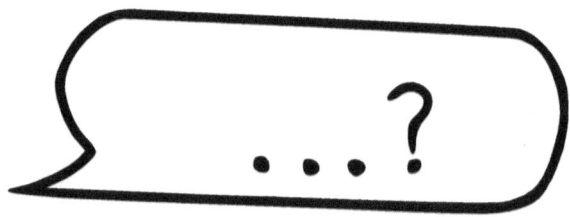

Come one, come all!
Check out the online speak!

CHAPTER 4

The New Language

I had no idea that I had to learn a new language to date online. I knew that the younger generations would use texting slang that would make me have to constantly google meanings, but I didn't know that a lot of that language would entail one-liners, words, stories, and phrases that could make you blush and turn hot, shake your head and smile, or run away like there was a five-alarm fire. There's a lot of smutty language in the world of online chatting. I suppose it's not really "new," but it definitely was to me. When I'd dated before my marriage, I met my boyfriend at work, and we didn't have the security of being risqué from the safety of cellphones.

Sometimes, I love some good dirt-ball texting—if I know the guy and we have a rapport. What the hell, right? I like to have fun and can be up for some sexting if I'm in a relationship with a man—and we're mostly stuck at home during a pandemic.

But some dudes were raunchy right from the get-go.

Calling me "sexy" or "hot" or a "MILF" wasn't going to win me over. Maybe if I had just been looking for phone sex? This new custom of dirty texting before you even know someone puts the cart before the horse. When their face is hidden behind a screen, some people will type *anything*. And perhaps there are some middle-aged, divorced women dating online who want this. I'm thinking there must be, because if it didn't work, guys would stop doing it. Right?

So up-front smut seems to be a thing, and I came to realize that if the messages were too crude too fast, the sex was more important to the guy than anything else. While sex is damn important, this was not the way to my heart. If I just wanted sex, sex toys work fine—and they don't talk back or have viruses! And that is sexy to me.

At least when it's dirty, there is actual communication. Although it's not the kind I wanted on the front end of finding my dream guy, at least there was something to giggle about. The new language doesn't just encompass filth and vulgar hilarity. It also entails a lack of communication and terms that describe what it means when there is silence when there should be talking.

The most surprising thing about dating today is the complete and utter disregard for good communication. The language of the online dating world has shifted to: "Let's see how little I can say, and how long I can wait to text back to keep 'em guessing." I mean, guys, you don't even have to talk on the phone right away. You can just use your damn thumbs to communicate. You can think about it, erase it, over and over, and deliberately send a perfect text that is thoughtful and appropriate. But no. I'm not sure if it's apathy, lack of true knowledge on how to talk to someone, or pure ego. Maybe it's stupidity? Could it possibly be entitlement? Or maybe it's good, old-fashioned laziness?

My favorite example of bad communication is the "hey guy." The introductory text that consists of a simple, yet ridiculous and nonmeaningful, hey.

HEY.

HEY.

That's it.

Not, "Hey there, how is your day going? I was thinking that we could plan something soon?" Or, "Good morning, hope you have a great day. Let's talk later." I started answering the "hey" texts with "hey back" because, honestly, I didn't know what I was supposed to say. (And I added "only says hey as an opening line" to my "deal breaker in a man" list.) Out of over 200 men I engaged with during my time online at least forty of them did this.

At the beginning of my online journey during the height of the lockdown in 2020, Justin was the first "hey guy," and because it was early on, I truly thought this was what I was going to have to deal with all the time. He wasn't the best communicator, and it looked like it stemmed from being shy. Being shy isn't a crime, but it was probably a sign he wasn't for me. Then others came along who started out with "hey," and I'd chuckle to myself remembering Justin the Hey Guy.

The concept of the "hey guy" became infamous among my pals. We were planning our first race since 2018 and decided that the front of our shirts needed to say something. Since this was still during COVID, we figured it would be a fun way to engage with the public while we ran by during our half marathon. For 13.1 miles we ran with "Hey" emblazoned on the front of our shirts. This homage to the hilarity of the lack of communication with men online turned into a huge amount of interaction during a race. People on the sidelines yelled "hey" to us for hours. The joy, laughter, and actual high-level of communication added to the irony of having our shirts emblazoned with a word that symbolized almost no communication. We discovered that the word *hey* says it all!

But honestly, "hey" is better than nothing when I think

how traumatizing it was when a guy was still seemingly "in the game" but would wait a considerable amount of time before checking in. It was hard to pick up on the proper text etiquette. If I was supposed to meet a guy for the first time tomorrow, I should probably have heard from him the day before. My intuition is strong, but this was a learning curve that took some time. If I hadn't heard anything by the day of our first date, I knew something was up. And I was right. I love being right in real life, but I hated how right I was in the online matrix. Blech. Being right in this world sucks.

The next term, *ghost,* is special. It can be a noun or a verb depending on use. But it's never a good thing. A ghost is no longer someone who haunts you after they have passed away, or someone in a Halloween costume trying to scare you. A ghost is someone who just stops texting without a word. No warning. No, "Hey, this isn't going to work because of this or that reason." Nothing—just gone. I would love to know when this became an acceptable thing: "Oh yeah, he ghosted me," or "Yeah, I didn't like him, so I ghosted him." Well, it's the biggest bunch of horseshit that goes with this crap show of a way to meet people.

The younger the man was, the more likely he was to ghost me, but it also happened with someone around my age. After two dates, two nights in a row—two nights of kissing goodnight, holding hands, movies at his house, and an exciting promise for date three—he was gone without a word.

Perhaps slipping away without warning when you're still on the app is fine. I've done that too. In the beginning, you don't owe much of a response during the first few exchanges. But honestly, when I was connecting with someone younger than forty, ghosting was almost normal. Perhaps they lost their nerve? Perhaps they didn't think I was real? Being behind a screen offers a lot of buffer and seems to justify dropping off without a word. But some would totally confuse me when they had seemed so excited at first. They'd say all the right things and then *poof*!

Ghosting seems to be a Generation Z word. Millennials are almost as old as I am, so I had to dip into my sons' age group to start a study session on how to interpret these assholes. All my younger clients say it's a totally acceptable thing to do. If you aren't interested into someone anymore, just stop talking to them without warning. *What?* Despite it being a "thing," it will never be one for me. Because we attract at a health level similar to our own, if I try to attract the type of person who is actually looking back at me in the mirror, I better feel good about what I see. And giving a proper goodbye creates the closure everyone needs, even on the other end of the internet.

My judgment is fierce when it comes to anyone who doesn't step away with class, so I always bowed out gracefully.

Heading down the Halloween-themed road of dating, the next term we find is *zombie*. You could liken it to *The Walking Dead* zombie, or the *Zombieland* zombie. Maybe even an old-school zombie like from *Dawn of the Dead* or *The Return of the Living Dead*. Regardless of the type of scary, ugly, undead, creeper you picture, the zombie of the dating world is just as terrifying, albeit he may still be sexy, dammit.

I was talking with someone I work with about her experience with online dating, and I mentioned a guy who had ghosted me and then, months later, came back. She said, "OMG, that guy is a zombie! Back from the proverbial dead in the online dating matrix."

I couldn't stop laughing. I said, "Well shit, I'm starting to feel like an expert." Not really an expertise I'm proud of, but an expert nonetheless. Ha.

So, a zombie is a ghost who comes back after a period of silence. The reasons for their return are varied:

I'm so sorry, I got back with my ex-girlfriend, but that didn't work out.

I lost my nerve to meet you, but I'm ready now.

I'm thinking about you today and hope you are well.

I was just watching that movie we watched together, and it made me think of you. How are you?

Sometimes they even dragged themselves back from the dead with the ever-popular "Hey!"

There isn't just one schema that explains a zombie, which is why the phenomenon keeps you hopping. But if you ask my pal Katy what's really going on, she will always tell the crass, hard truth. "Rose, they just want to get their dick wet. Decide if that is all you want too." Ha. The gospel according to Katy. All should listen. All should learn. She speaks the truth. But that has never been all that I want.

I did have a favorite zombie. Stu the Drummer texted and ghosted and texted and ghosted so many times it became a game of sorts. We had an amazing first date. I stuck to my "no sex on the first date" rule, and we just had a great time connecting. He talked about helping my kid on the drums, seeing me again that weekend, and how he wanted to text me pictures of his night out with his friends. And then he was gone. *Gone.* By this time, I had become accustomed to having zero expectations and not counting my chickens before they hatch, but shit, this one annoyed me. Even when you lower your hopes to zero, you're not a damn robot. My feelings were hurt.

He showed up again six months later, only to leave again six more times. Or was it seven? The first time he reappeared, he told me our age difference had bothered him, and he'd gotten scared. But we'd had such an amazing evening together that he wanted to try again. He was dirty—called me his queen and told me he wanted me to sit on his face and ride him. That he craved me. That he needed me. But Stu also seemed to mean well and was very sweet. He had goals and hopes and dreams and always apologized sincerely for being scared off. He always had an explanation and always begged for another chance. I wonder what it was about me that was so hypnotizing yet so untouchable and intimidating? I mean, I know I'm cute and successful, but am I "all that"? Apparently yes, and a bag of chips.

So, my friends and I would read his texts, expect less than nothing, and smile and shake our heads. Katy would say, "Oh, Stu," and we would set a date, only for him to be gone again without a word. Bye, Stu.

"Hey, ladies, guess who's back?"

"OMG! Stu?"

"Yep."

The last round also earned him a "hey" spot, since that's how he started his text.

I can't explain the pull to keep going back to him. I was just so intensely curious about what he saw in me that made him continue to come back, only to get scared again. *Who is this guy, and what is going on?*

Rose, I mean it this time. I did a lot of soul searching, and I'm ready to date.

So we planned another date. I waited for him that night. Nothing. Gone again without a word or a breath or a song. Fool me once, shame on you. Fool me twice, three times, seven times, eight times? Shame, shame, shame on me!

Thank goodness I had learned not to count my chickens, because, man, did this one test my ability to keep my wits about me and my expectations at subzero. But he did earn the "ten-time zombie-gone-hey-guy" award, and any award is something to be proud of. Bravo, Stu the Drummer. You earned something shiny in the world of stupidity and ridiculous. Congratulations, sweet guy.

I finally blocked him. He became my most infamous zombie.

———

Language is a funny thing. Every time you learn the latest slang word, the most politically correct word, or the most current way to write, things change on you. You can grow up with all the proper grammar in the world, but language changes and twists and becomes outdated so quickly. I had to listen hard to my seventeen-year-old to know what slang is for what. But one thing is certain, the language of finding love will never be easy. And when the other person isn't really a "person" at first but a figment on the other side of a screen, it's easy to forget that it's not about you if they go away. It's about them. And if you're the kind of person who can't even say goodbye or more than "hey," do I really want you anyway?

Fuck no.

The clowns get the biggest, juiciest
laughs, then leave.

CHAPTER 5

It's All Funny

Joan Rivers once said, "Life goes by fast. Enjoy it. Calm down. It's all funny." Wow, does this resonate with me now. Of course, not everything is funny. So many things are insulting, demeaning, unbelievably rude, horrifying, disgusting, repulsive, sad, angering, and downright stupid. Tragedies and traumas challenge Rivers' words. Hard loss combined with grief pushes at the boundaries of their meaning. But in my mind, Rivers meant to say, "I know things can be hard, but we have to keep laughing as much as we can, or we will drown in our sadness and pain."

Humor is my coping skill. Sometimes I even use it at extremely inappropriate times to take the edge off the intensity of what is going on. While I know sometimes things are not at all funny, trying to find the humor however we can changes everything.

When I finally stopped taking this dating stuff so seriously and lowered my expectations to zero, I made a decision:

for every interaction I decided to talk about (because some came and went so fast, I couldn't even remember them), my friends and I would laugh our asses off about it. Humor changed everything. In life you must decide how you are going to interpret what is coming at you, and then you can decide if you want to cry and internalize the insults or laugh and know that, as long as you're on a dating app, there will always be another one.

Max the Contractor contacted me after a long hiatus.

Sorry about that. That first date with you was fun, but then I gave my ex-girlfriend another try, and it didn't work out, so I wanted to know if you wanted to go out again.

We talked about his radio silence (ghosting), his returning out of the blue (hello, zombie), and how I wouldn't tolerate that again. He agreed, asked me out again, only to disappear —again. Funny!

Sam the Football Player texted for a couple of days and then sent:

I'll talk to you tomorrow.

I texted him the next day to say good morning and . . . nothing. At 8:00 p.m. that evening, I texted: "Did you change your mind, Sam?" He said nope. And I replied, "You could say hi!" Later that night he texted, "You're being needy, Rose. That's a turn off." How my wanting a quick "hello" text from him just to show me he was still interested meant that I was needy, I'll never understand. Perhaps the person I was at the beginning of this journey would have been pissed as hell. Instead, I laughed until I actually peed! *Needy? This couldn't be furthest from the truth. I texted back:*

I was just having fun, but take care. Bye!

So comical! I'm still chuckling.

Chris, a guy closer to my age, arrived fifteen minutes late for our first date, apologizing because his massage ran over. Then, without asking me one question, he proceeded to brag about his motorcycles, his cars, his newly remodeled home, and his perfect children. After the worst kiss of my life—a little too slobbery and absolutely zero finesse (yes, I know, why did I kiss him?)—I texted him two days later, saying he must have had the same feelings about our connection (negative) since I hadn't heard from him. He texted back: "Oh, I had a great time, but I guess you didn't." Yeah, dude, you had fun with yourself. Because that's who you dated two nights ago with all your self-talk: yourself! Silly stuff.

Blue-Eyed Cody was so intimidated by me he couldn't even look at me. This guy looked up, down, or sideways the entire date. I only knew he had blue eyes because of his pictures. Too bad. He was sweet, kind, cute. And afraid. Very afraid! Crazy—and kind of funny.

Steve the Social Worker was super nice. We had a great dinner and tons of conversation since we had social work in common. But he was so newly divorced, he hadn't read the dating handbook yet. You know, the part in the first chapter that says it's not necessary to tell your first date every single detail about your divorce and your living situation. Oh, I got an earful. After our date, I texted: "I'd love to go out again." He replied, "Just so you know, I'm talking to *many* women right now." *What? Okay, Steve. You're not all that.* And really, the proverbial handbook also tells you not to say *everything* that's in your head. Of course, we aren't exclusive; but dude, keep it to yourself! I suggested he contact me when he knew what he wanted. I never heard back. Silly guy who doesn't know the rules yet. Bye, Steve!

Then there was Michael, the sweet guy whom I really started to like. He was thirty-nine years old and drove forty-five minutes for our first date. There was definite chemistry. He had lived in Vietnam for ten years, teaching English and doing philanthropic work. He'd been super nice on the phone, texted and communicated, and was very interesting. He'd never been married and didn't have kids, but this didn't register as a red flag. After all, he'd been out of the country so long, focusing on his work. I thought, *Wow, obviously no baggage with this one—obviously* being the key word here. We talked a lot at dinner, we swung on the swing on my back deck, and we had a great little make-out session. We planned on seeing each other again.

While we were planning our next date, it became apparent that his mother, whom he had been living with since returned to the States, was the infamous baggage I thought I was avoiding. He had returned home to help care for her, and she was being demanding of his time, didn't want him to use her car, and got upset that he had been out with a friend. The morning of the date, thirty minutes before we were to meet, she told him "If you go, you don't love me." He canceled right there and then—and I was in the middle of cooking lunch for us. He said his mom came first.

At first I was sad and disappointed, but then I just had to laugh. Having a thirty-nine-year-old man cancel a date because his mommy wouldn't let him come was just so ridiculous.

My friend Kevin (of the "no chickens" rule) and I spent hours together, chuckling about our bad dates and coining terms that made us laugh out loud. Kevin would bust out with a one-liner like, "Tomfoolery knows no age limits," meaning even older guys would treat me poorly when we'd thought the issue with another was his youth.

We laughed about how there were more fish in the pond for him since he's bisexual. But it also meant he had more crazy fish to choose from: more doesn't always mean better and crazy just meant there were more to throw back in. Kevin wondered what kind of crazy he would find next and whether it had anything to do with gender. The answer? Not really. Crazy comes in all types, and Kevin's stories rivaled mine.

Through all the false starts and hopes when we would start dating someone, Kevin and I felt we were on the job. As therapists, we guided our dates toward healthier communication. We taught them that they should text more; that they really should pay for dinner, at least every other date; that they should listen to what the other person wanted. Sometimes, things would get better for a while with one of the people we were dating, and we felt as though we were truly showing them the ways to healthier, fun relationships. But then they'd go away. They left for various reasons. Once, after a month of dating, a guy told me he "wasn't feeling the vibe" anymore. What in the actual hell does that mean? Another guy said that while it was all fun, he really wasn't looking for "anything regular." With yet another, things were going well, but we knew our age difference would get in the way, so we decided to remain casual.

These casual dates often turned into teaching lessons for both Kevin and me, and that's when we coined the term *dating foster parents*: We taught our dates. We showed them the ropes. We coached them. Then they went to their forever homes. Their future partners should thank us for the work we put in. We trained them: from their ability to text back to their new talents in the bedroom. You're so damn welcome. As Kevin and I explained to all our friends what *dating foster parent* meant, the ensuing side-splitting laughter combined with knowing nods helped us believe that we were, in fact, some pretty kickass teachers. Since I teach as part of my day job, we joked about my offering a workshop on how to foster casual dates to help them become amazing life partners for someone else.

But sometimes it can be hard to laugh and make fun when you're dealing with lying, being stood up, being treated in a way you wouldn't treat your worst enemy. But laughter helped my mental health in a way it couldn't have withstood otherwise and was imperative for survival in the woods of the internet.

Lying was the toughest thing to laugh at. My profile stated that I needed a phone call, that I wanted someone to *actually date*—not just have sex with. And I always asked up front if the age difference was okay, because I was often matched with men in their thirties. They always said yes: "Age is just a number." "You don't look your age anyway." "The age difference is fine with me." I reminded them that I wasn't going to have more children and that many previous men had said the age difference was okay only to cancel our date after talking for a week, because "I thought about it, and the age difference does bother me." It was incredible how many men would say, "I'm not that guy," only to be that guy!

There was one guy who, after our second date, promised he was very interested. We had laughed and had a lot of fun together. Five days of silence went by, only to finally hear from him: "Dating you reminded me that I'm not over my ex-girlfriend. I figured that out after you left." *What*? Right before I left, we'd planned our next date. What happened in the minutes in between? An epiphany? A spiritual awakening? A religious experience? I doubt it. I think he lied. Sigh.

Were they lying up front? It's hard to say. Why would anyone deliberately waste their own time? Maybe their balls shrunk in the time we talked? I think some of them forgot I was a real person with a real life. To them, I was just a pretty picture—until I wasn't.

One guy and I messaged for a couple of weeks as he'd gone on vacation between us matching and setting a time for our first date. He was younger than the men I usually dated, so I was extremely up front—again. I told him we didn't need to be serious, but that I did want to date monogamously and to have a good time. He said he was "all in!" The first clue should have been that he wanted to communicate on Snapchat, which was new to me. The younger guys who wanted all evidence of sending a picture to be gone as soon as it was seen usually liked "snapping": talking, texting, and sharing pictures that just disappear when the conversation is over. No remnants. No reminders. I ignored my intuition, which my friend Christie says is rock solid (shame on me), and went out with him. We had a good time, but after our date he messaged:

> You really think I wanted more than one date? You're kidding yourself.

Dammit, another liar! But I laughed, knowing it was just as much my fault as his because I had sensed it wouldn't work and ignored my gut.

———

Again and again, I kept trying to fit a square peg into a round hole. Because I *wanted* someone. But I started to learn that playtime was over, and I had to get serious about being serious. My laughter may have been a great coping skill, but perhaps I really did want something more serious than I was advertising. I guess I should have considered it a relief when guys blew me off before a date, or even after a date, before I invested more of my feelings, emotions, and time.

I realize that finding the funny in someone lying to you is a difficult task. But the more you laugh, the more you stay sane. And the saner you are, the more likely you can go back in for more. Because going back for more is the way to find the man who will hopefully end the game, turn it into something real, and turn the real into something special. In the meantime, like your visits to the circus, sit back, laugh, enjoy the show, and know that you can always walk out the door and come back when you're ready again.

My advice is to stop being sad and hurt about the lying, the fostering, the manipulative moms, the egotistical dudes, the intimidated ones, the overly open social-worker types, and all those in between. Take a breath, shake your head, and start laughing. Cause really? It's all funny.

Intermission

This chapter break is brought to you by the letter *C* for "contacts," and the number 101 for the number of men on the list. I didn't date them all, but this is how I kept track of who came into my phone from the app. These men were known by their nicknames, which were a way to chuckle at the madness.

Anthony the
   Young and Dumb
Anthony the Young
Stu the Drummer
Max the Drummer (so
   many drummers)
Justin Music
Tyler EMT
Tyler Dirt Ball
Phil P.
Samson the Marine
Ethan Super Young

Jay the Surprise
Aaron the Marine
Aaron Scorpio
Adam Spiritual
Adam Tattoo/Music
Alex Attorney
Andrew Sexy
Anthony Gorgeous Eyes
Anthony Nice Arms
Anthony Rugged
Brady Young
Brett Doctor

Ben Beard (spoiler alert,
this one turned into Ben
with a Heart)

Cam Sweet Young One

Cary the Babe

Casey Conservative (Yikes!
What was I thinking?)

Charles the Lifter

Chase Blue Eyes Hipster

Chris the Jewish Guy

Chris the Musician

Chris the Bodybuilder

Chuck Personal Trainer

Clayton Lips

Cody Tattoos

Cody Blue Eyes

Colin EMT

Colin Lawyer/Artist

Jewish Jake

Jordan Hockey

Corey Hippie

Craig Finance

Danny Woodworker

Danny Guitar

David Beer Guy

Dustin PhD Student

Ed-Curly

Eric Ginger

Jacob Beard

Jake Cross-Fit

Jake Young

Jake Sexy Kisser

James Long Island

Stan Germany

Jeff Ice

Jimmy Young

Joe German Shepherd

Joe Ultra-Runner

Joe Young Hottie

Jon Motorcycle

Jonathan Young

Jon Hot Kisser

Justin Green Eyes

Matt Hot

Matt Respiratory Therapist

Matt Sexy

Matt the Cutie

Mat the Contractor

Michael Older

Michael Blond

Mike Young Dead-Lifter

Mitch Hockey

Mitch Young Financial

Mitchell

Monte the Golf Pro

Nate Engineer

Nate Country Boy

Nathaniel the Power Lifter

Nick Lawyer

Nick Recovery

Nick Sweet Young Guy

Nick Fashion/Husky

Pablo

Patrick Blue Eyes

Philip Muscles

Ray San Diego

Rocco Italian

Ross PR Guy

Ross Smile

Ryan Cute

Ryan OSU

Tyler Young

Scott 33-Year-Old

Shawn Blue Eyes

Spencer Young

Steve Social Services

Tom the 31-Year-Old

Tommy Young-ish

Thomas New Zealand

Tyler Glasses

Vince Lawyer

Walt Horses

Will Green-Blue Eyes

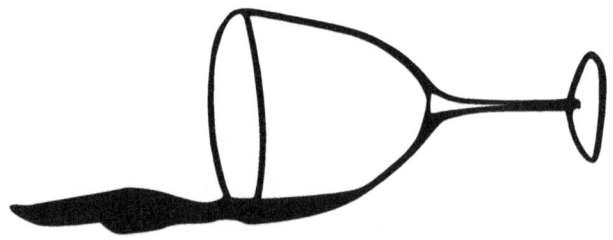

Built to amaze, built to astonish—
but age still matters.

CHAPTER 6

Cougar Time

In the circus, you see a lot of acrobatics with ropes and tricks that amaze and astonish you. Sometimes, you'll see contortionists doing a type of limbo, leaning back and scooting under a pole that gets lower and lower. The flexibility needed to bend and the talent needed to scoot can be difficult but entertaining in the online dating world as well.

Deciding on the age of the men I was willing to date put me in a limbo of sorts. My mantras became: "How low will I go?" and "How casual will I go?" I was game for being casual but monogamous, but I wasn't looking for friends-with-benefits or one-night stands.

Most of the men my age were on the hunt for a wife, and I noticed that many of them had let themselves go down Alice in Wonderland's proverbial rabbit hole with a bag of Cheetos, a twelve-pack of beer, and a very large La-Z-Boy. The men in their thirties seemed okay at first, but often proved to be scared little bunnies, afraid of even casual commitment, afraid of communication, and afraid of their own shadows. Perhaps there was a reason they were still single?

Men in their twenties? I'm not embarrassed to admit that I decided to play in that pond for a bit. I mean, why not? I knew that it would be casual and, after decades of marriage, letting my "inner slut" out seemed well deserved and something I wanted to try. I got married when I was twenty-four years old, and it had been a long time since I'd navigated this game of attraction. But doing so during a pandemic? To avoid a deadly virus of the COVID kind, or any other viruses of the sexually transmitted kind, the questions became a version of: Where has your face been, where has your dick been?

Since young men, overall, seemed willing to date older women with the assumption it wouldn't get serious, it looked like my ticket to a casual relationship. On the app, I lowered the age range of men I was willing to meet, got out my popcorn and wine, and watched as younger guys started flocking to me like moths to flames.

Often a guy would talk to me for days, telling me details and about his interests, only to say, "You know what? The age difference does matter." Or they'd say they wanted the same things only to "change their minds" after the first date. It appears the bravery and curiosity behind the phone often didn't extend to the face-to-face date, and many couldn't put their money where their mouths was when they had to meet me. I had to be willing to risk all of this when heading down into the lower age ranges. And like a circus act, sometimes it was daring, most of the time it was alluring, but many times it ended in disappointment. It's your prerogative and choice on whether or not you're willing to risk the bad for the good, since the good is so often fleeting. "Living in the date" became the motto for this age range, since the one date is often where it stopped.

Why the attraction to an older woman? Apparently, I am a MILF. I mentioned the term *MILF* earlier, but it deserves its own discussion because being a MILF has many implications. If you're not familiar with this modern-day acronym, it means "mother I'd like to fuck," meaning you're still hot at a certain age. But is that a good thing? I'm told it is.

This is also when I started to wonder if I officially fit the label of a *cougar*? Urban Dictionary defines a cougar as "an older woman who frequents clubs to score with a much younger man. The cougar can be anyone from an overly surgically altered wind tunnel victim, to an absolute sad and bloated old horn-meister, to a real hottie or MILF. Cougars are gaining in popularity—particularly the true hotties—as young men find not only a sexual high, but many times a chick with her shit together."

If it was good enough for Demi Moore, would it be okay for me? Would I now be considered the kind of dirt ball I myself was trying to avoid? What would people think of me, and did I care? Being called a "cougar" doesn't sound like a compliment. Younger men often consider it a conquest, and it all becomes a game. Older women often feel it means they still look "hot" and wear it like a badge. I couldn't decide how I felt, but I knew if I was going into the ring as a cougar, I was going to have to own it.

Months later, I got a tattoo of an actual cougar: a creature who leads without force, has a balanced disposition, and combines power and protectiveness with strength and survival. The female cougar carries herself as if she were a goddess and will battle ferociously to protect her young. I've always had strong convictions, unwavering faith in myself and my intuition, and self-assuredness in my actions. I'm fiercely loyal and protective. So for me, the deeper meaning behind a cougar being "a hot older woman with a younger man," was that she is fierce with goddess-like qualities. When I stepped into this act of the show, I held my head high and decided I would own it like the boss I am.

I researched why older women were interested in younger men. After all, there had to reasons for this label. Higher libidos and being in better shape than many middle-aged men were some of the items on the list, along with a way to feel in control of the date. Often, because of the age difference, the woman is the one who picks the restaurant and what happens afterward.

I decided being a cougar and dating younger men felt safe in a strange way. If I dated someone I could never picture myself with in the long term, I could easily guard my feelings. So, I did indeed fish in the forbidden pond. I had some fun, and knew I deserved it. After a broken marriage and a year with a broken leg, I knew part of my healing was to see who was out there, and I could decide later what I wanted long term. If it wasn't meant to be, it wasn't going to hurt me, and I could let myself have some fun for a bit. Fun without strings? I gave it a whirl—but no one-night stands.

Except? I did make one exception to that rule. Jake was a twenty-eight-year-old who'd never been with an older woman, and he was honest and forthcoming about his intentions up front: "I can't promise anything past one date." His honesty hooked me, and I decided he would be the one guy I'd be with for a night, with no promises, no strings attached. The communication was clear and honest—and the texting was dirty. And I mean super dirty. When we met, he was incredibly sweet, very honest, totally sexy, and we had some safe fun. I protected my feelings and the next day felt pretty damn triumphant that I didn't feel like a dirt ball.

He messaged me thirty-six hours later.

My friends told me I'd be a donkey-brained fool to not ask for another night. You're so amazing.

Well, well, well, wasn't that a surprise! And I obliged. Two more times!

With the young ones, it was shocking to me what many of them would say to begin a conversation and how fast pictures of their naked bodies would fly onto my phone. Maybe I'd made a mistake considering dating the young? Maybe it was because the world was a bit strange during this time? But I digress—who am I to even know what it was like before COVID? All I know is that by week two of talking to these younger ones, the offers of sex in the woods were coming so quickly, I had to continually reevaluate what in the actual hell I was doing. I knew if I wanted to just play, I could set a wide age range. But was that even me? Could I casually date at all? Was it even responsible in these times? My standard answer to "what are you looking for" became this: "I want something real. I want it to be monogamous. But it doesn't have to be serious. Just whatever happens naturally." This caught a bunch of fish. But not always the right kind. As an apparent glutton for punishment, I dove into the world of "not needing to be serious, but let's go to dinner." Could my feelings handle this? How thick was my skin? How strong was my armor? Because young men seem to feed your self-esteem initially and then step on it eventually.

A few months into my dating career, I met Nathaniel the Power Lifter. He seemed to have his head on straight, even if he was twenty-eight years young. He was finishing college and wanted to become a social worker. He wasn't dating other women and agreed that, if we hit it off, we'd date exclusively. We followed the rules of texting, then a phone call, and then a proper date to feel out the chemistry. After our first date, I decided he wasn't for me, but it was also then that I realized young didn't have to mean dumb, and that younger, or older, didn't mean better.

My girlfriends and I laughed a lot about how low I was willing to go, and they wondered what the intimacy was like. In bed, I found out that younger doesn't mean better and that most of the young ones needed some serious guidance. They were less experienced, more self-focused, and truly dumb when it came to what to do with a woman's body. Sexy but stupid. Pretty to look at, bad at the rest. And paying for dinner? Rarely.

———

Feelings can seep out the sides of the armor like lava, and when this happens, it can burn. Stan the German and Anthony the Young and Dumb took me to dinner. Both claimed they wanted a girlfriend—the middle. Someone to have fun with but not necessarily get serious with. But after a couple of dates, they both decided age did indeed matter, but they were sorry they'd wasted my time.

I was very clear with Stan about what I wanted. He acted like this would be perfect for him. He told me that he was traveling a lot that summer, so having someone to casually date would work for him, as he didn't want to get serious or too attached when he was going back and forth to Europe. He made a big deal about how brilliant the idea of having the "middle" was and went so far as to say that he had been wanting something like that for a long time. Date one went really well, and we went from a bar to a restaurant quickly. I drove my car for safety reasons, and his goodnight kiss started inside of the restaurant and ended on the sidewalk. The next day the infamous text came. "I changed my mind, I decided that your age does bother me."

Charles the Lifter canceled each of the three dates we'd planned. The infamous nine-time, or was it ten-time, zombie Stu the Drummer was also young. He continued to plan dates and then get scared. Plan and scared. Plan and scared. Always about the age difference. They all liked the idea of dating a cougar, but chickened out in the end. They'd forget that I was a real person with feelings on the other end of the phone.

Just when I started thinking that younger men were just ego-stroking, pretty faces, I ran into a good one. He was twenty-six. Yes, you heard that right. Judge away for me earning my cougar status, but what I've learned from this crazy circus is that there are assholes and good guys of all ages. The good ones are confident and clear about their feelings and where they see the relationship going.

Twenty-six-year-old Aaron the Marine was a good guy. We met in January 2021, during the height the pandemic. We both needed some distraction and connection. We talked openly about how, eventually, he'd be looking for a woman closer to his age. He wanted to move south, and a wife and kids were a significant part of his plan. We knew I wasn't his forever girl, but we also knew we were dating in strange times. Could I keep to my rule of having a casual-but-real thing? Could I be his "for now girl?" More than friends-with-benefits but not fall for him? Aaron and I agreed that if we met someone else, we would tell the other person first. We both wanted some low-key companionship and some good communication and intimacy.

I did well—but he didn't. We had fun. A lot of fun. It lasted five months. After dinner one night, when we'd gone back to my house, he said, "I feel like it's becoming too hard to keep this casual. I'm developing real feelings for you." That is when I knew we had to stop. If Aaron was to move on with his plans, we couldn't allow real feelings to win out. It was proof that sometimes casual can become serious.

———

What did I learn from this crazy and gutsy circus act? That dating a young man in a casual way can be done, but you've got to remember to watch your feelings and have your support team back you without judgment. Make sure the communication is clear and honest. I told myself going in that it would be a time to have relaxed fun and avoid any expectations of commitment. Sowing my oats was important in that phase of my post-marriage dating time. My friends, being a constant sounding board and reminding me to have fun and what this time was for, helped me a lot.

Perhaps the men didn't have this type of support, so their armor was weaker. But support is crucial if you're going to keep your nerve up and your armor in place. If you think you can do connection, friendship, and intimacy without allowing yourself to fall deeply in love, know that maybe you can, or maybe you can't. Either way, it's a learning curve, and you'll discover if dating younger men is for you. My ego may have taken some hits, but it was also boosted up high. That, combined with good food and a lot of fun, can give you what you need during a time in your life when you're just not sure what you're looking for. And as this act in the ring came to an end, my need for this type of experience ended. Having this time to break from the pressure of finding "the one" seemed to create space in my heart again. And with this ending, came a readiness for something more serious, with a possibility of forever.

Don't blame a clown for acting like a clown.
Ask yourself why you keep going
to the circus.

CHAPTER 7

Don't Count Your Chickens

I've told you how my friend Kevin and I had the rule of not counting our chickens before they hatched, but I want to expand on what happens to your hopes, expectations, excitement, and feelings when you adopt this mantra while in the online dating world. It's important to highlight what it can look like to work hard to manage your feelings. The excitement and hope that can come from one initial connection needs to be harnessed, held back, and put in a box for longer than you would think. Even after a couple of good dates, someone can vanish, leaving as fast as they came, with no explanation. The ups and downs of this ride are like the El Loco roller coaster at Circus Circus: a ninety-foot ascent, followed by negative drops and 180 degree turns that will make your stomach weak. Dating online felt like the anxious anticipation of the ascent and then the terrifying fear of the decent, all coupled with the thrill of high expectations when you sometimes get stuck with a nauseous stomach and emotional frustration that it wasn't what it was advertised to be.

This happened with several of the men I talked to, and the letdown that happened after a few dates, or even a month of dating, brought on the online dating trauma: getting back on the roller coaster, hoping this time will be better, while guarding your feelings against a bad descent.

I got so good at guarding my feelings that when something good and real came along, I was in protection mode—like the cougar with her cubs—and no one was getting past my barriers. I had to unlearn so much, but having the mantra, "don't count your chickens" still stood. Only it got harder to tell when the eggs hatched, since sometimes they did, but then the baby chickens flew the coop.

I dated Jordan for a month, and he seemed like a good egg. There wasn't any dirty talk up front; he cared deeply for his kids, whom he had 50 percent of the time; he had a good job; and we were both Jewish. Our initial conversations were about Jewish geography—when two Jews meet, they find out who they know in common. We laughed about how our mothers worried and how excited they would be to know we were talking to another Jewish person as a prospective partner. These commonalities, along with an understanding that we both were busy but liked daily texts, gave me a good feeling.

Stocky, short, and very hairy, he wasn't the most traditionally attractive guy, and being a dad who'd gone through a tough divorce made him seem older than his years. I decided that his younger age was worth a chance since he was older in spirit. We met for drinks for our first date and kissed goodnight. The conversation was easy, and the kiss was the perfect tongue-to-lip ratio—nothing sloppy. I felt my stomach drop a little. I knew the chemistry was there and was hopeful that it would be the start of something real.

After a few dates, we called it off because of scheduling conflicts, only to reconnect a month later since we'd both been thinking about each other. Then I met his kids, and we spent more time together. We had an incredibly good connection, the right balance between carefree and serious, and we seemed to get along well. But then, one evening just seemed "off." When I asked what was going on, he said he'd been thinking about our possible future, and our age difference was starting to bother him. We had a great conversation about it and agreed to keep dating, recognizing that the scheduling conflicts could be worked through if he was willing for me to be around his children more. We realized we had a great physical connection and the conversation flowed easily. When he told me that he had been thinking about me at the exact moment I reached out to him, I knew this deserved another shot. Meeting someone's small children early in a developing relationship isn't common. But Jordan reconsidered his ability to spend time with me, and three days later, we had a night out with the kids at the movies. Everything seemed to be going great—and the sex was mind blowing. I was starting to think I'd found the perfect "real" scenario, until one night, when I asked him if he was coming over, he said we needed to talk. He was no longer "feeling the vibe."

Feeling the vibe? What?

I told him he had certainly been feeling the vibe the previous night when I was naked on his couch. "Yeah," he replied, "I'm sorry. I was trying to see if one more date would change my mind, but it didn't."

While he had the decency to tell me about it over the phone instead of ghosting me, that's where the decency ended. He could have warned me he was investigating our "vibe" before he decided to sleep with me again. I said to him, "Please don't do this to another woman."

I'd let my barriers down after that month and then? The lack of vibe. It's a Millennial thing this Gen Xer doesn't get. If he was "vibing" with me for a month, what happened? Jordan was a chicken I was counting, and then he was gone.

———

My pals and I are constantly confused. I mean, we have learned to have no expectations except the expectation to expect nothing. And to remember that nothing matters until it matters. Nothing. But sometimes we were still surprised. Or disappointed?

I went on a date with Anthony the Young, who seemed different. And whenever I say that now, I think to myself, *Girl, you know better.* Coming off the cougar chapter, I'm embarrassed to admit I was again pulled into believing that a relationship could work with someone significantly younger than me. He complimented who I was, not what I looked like—although he did say, over and over, how cute I was. We texted for a few days, then he came over a day ahead of our planned date since he "couldn't wait." I broke my rule about seeing him at my house before the first date, and we got to know each other a bit before our official first date the following night. I'm not sure what created a comfort level that allowed me to tell him my address. As I sit here now, I'm embarrassed by that decision. My intuition was messy, since he was saying things in a way no one had before. I kept my chicken eggs in their coop, nervously waiting to see if he would pick me up on time. He surprised me by showing up when he said he would.

Our date followed a different script than many of the other dates. He was following through and doing things no other date had. He disarmed me with his charm, took me to a beautiful outdoor downtown spot with an expensive menu. He planned it all, picked me up, and paid the bill, which must have been close to $200. We had really good chemistry. When he dropped me off, he said he would text me the next day. I chuckled to myself as I got out of the car, thinking there was a fifty-fifty chance of him following through for a second date. Even if things seemed to be going well, the age difference loomed in my head. But my chicken eggs were screaming to leave the coop as I felt my excitement grow and my expectations trying to break free.

No text the next day. The day after that, he took me off the dating app, which means he deleted my profile so I couldn't see his anymore. This meant one of two things: he was only interested in dating me and had left the app altogether, or he'd deleted me because he wasn't interested. It's a mean thing to do, because before they even tell you they're gone, they show you they are.

It really stung when he eventually called me and said that he wasn't over his last girlfriend, but that I'd helped him to realize that. *Lovely. Glad to be of service to a story that is probably not even true.* I decided it didn't matter—that nothing mattered—and I pulled myself back together. Usually, I took one day to be sad and pissed, and then I moved on and kept my chicken eggs close.

So I moved from one date to the next, one conversation on the app to one on the phone, and one phone call to the next. Although it was difficult, discouraging, and stressful, my desire to find something real outweighed the need to take a break. If it got to be too difficult on my heart, I would stop, but my fiercely determined spirit, combined with a new desire to almost *prove* there was someone out there in the male form, but like me, kept me in the ring.

Jon the Hot Kisser, a redheaded firecracker, met me for dinner, and we split the check. We made out in my car for an hour. We hit it off, planned a date for three days later, and we texted a lot in between. *Oh, can I count my chickens yet?* He texted me up to one hour before our next date, and then he no-showed. Yep. He didn't show despite texting an hour beforehand. He finally responded to my questioning texts the next day:

> I came home from work and fell asleep on the floor while taking my shoes off.

He told me how sorry he was and that he'd make it up to me. *Yeah, Jon, I highly doubt that.* That text hit a new level, and I applauded him for his creativity—bullshit creativity but creativity nonetheless. I told him I wasn't interested in his "making it up to me," because I knew the chances were slim to none, and I didn't feel like being hopeful that day. Falling asleep on the floor while taking your shoes off. WTAF?

Eric the Ginger—another redhead—and I never met in person. We talked on the phone a lot, and he made me laugh so hard I had tears running down my face, and my cheeks hurt. It was tax season, and he claimed he couldn't meet me for a while due to his job. But we texted and chatted, and he seemed like a fun guy. In his quirky way, he was endearing. He explained his failed relationships, that he'd never been married, had no kids, and was in his older thirties. I started to get hopeful, but stepped back, since it seemed as though we'd never actually meet. It's hard to tell what happened with this one, but I stepped away because if someone really wanted to meet me, they would. So much wasted time and emotional energy. After this one, I learned to meet the potential chickens quickly, or no investment. Damn chickens.

Thomas the New Zealander lived an hour away and traveled half the year. I thought that might bode well: we could date for a few months, and then he'd have to leave. I wouldn't get too attached. But damn if he wasn't fun during our conversations. We texted and laughed together on the phone and decided this would be a perfect monogamous-but-casual set up. After a few dinner dates, he came over to watch a movie. As I put my glasses on, he called me grandma and made fun of my age. He thought he was being funny, but he'd gone too far. When he left, I knew I was cutting him off. I texted him a nice closure text, and he said he believed I'd be back. *Sorry, Thomas, I'm good. Really. Bye.* No problem keeping my chicks in the coop on that one.

Justin the Musician was sexy. He was in his early thirties, taught at a university two hours away, and had partial custody of his small child. He called me on his way home from class one day, and our conversation was funny and interesting. He invited me to dinner at a local place with great drinks and fancy food, and we sat at a cute outside table.

Justin was kind to the server—a must—and his tone was flirty, in a good way. We shared stories of our horrible dates, and I thought a chicken was about to hatch. I figured if Justin and I were both talking about dating fails, there'd be an unspoken commitment to not act like a fool. But I told that would-be hatchling to pipe down before we got too excited.

Justin's kiss goodnight was pretty mind blowing, and he waltzed away with a kooky confidence, saying, "See you next time." We texted each other that same night, and it seemed we were both on the same page about our second date. But alas, it never happened. He canceled twice, saying that his schedule was busy, and he couldn't help it. As a single mom with two boys myself, many jobs, and a household to manage, I understood *busy*. But when you set a date and time, it's an unwritten contract that you aren't busy enough to see me again, and when you date on a dating app, I'm assuming that means you want to date. Silly me, what a mistake to assume anything logical. I told him that canceling two times was disrespectful to my time, and he ghosted into the unknown.

Max the Contractor—also known as an infamous zombie —was incredibly respectful, played nice, texted back, and took me out for a nice dinner. He is what I like to call a ghost disguised as a nice guy—with his sweater vest, his good job, and his love of golf. It's not that I cared much about this one after date one, but he seemed like a nice guy, and nice guys are so rare, I got a teeny bit hopeful. But nope, he was gone after a few texts about how great our date was.

By now I was getting good at this, and as minor disappointment set in, I looked back to the app for new dudes. With Max I felt like I had learned how to hold my clutch close, so my heart was nice and safe.

Craig the Finance Guy was the toughest one of the

counting-your-chickens bunch. On our first date, we talked nonstop about real life: work, kids, music, and our past relationships. He discussed his ex-wife in a way that sounded like they split amicably with an understanding that feelings change. I was slightly curious about how easy he'd made it sound, but on the first date, I didn't like to elaborate a lot on the past. He mentioned that he hadn't had a date like ours in a long time. The eye contact we had across the table threw my intuition that he liked me into high gear. I thought, *Wow, this feels like a normal, nice, cool dude. Wonder what happened in his last relationship?* We had a quick kiss goodnight, and when I got home and texted him how much fun I'd had, he responded immediately that we should meet at his house the next night.

When I got there, he showed me around, and we talked about our kids some more. After dinner, we watched a movie, and he held my hand. After our kiss goodnight and texts about meeting again for a third date, my clutch was getting excited. This fifty-two-year-old guy with a great job, a nice house, a daughter he was dedicated to, who'd kissed me goodnight and talked about date three ghosted me the next day. He took me off the app and was gone.

It was this type of behavior from men that made me start losing trust in my own intuition, and the online dating trauma I mentioned earlier continued to surface as my time in the circus dragged on. As I tried desperately to remember not to count my chickens, this self-protection eventually jaded me. I pride myself on being optimistic, although this was certainly a challenge in the two years after my broken leg and divorce. I tried to find balance in holding back my feelings while remaining hopeful after two successful dates and talk of a third.

In time, these punches to the gut felt less hurtful as I met new men. With help and support from my friends, my self-esteem remained intact; and my curiosity about the whole online process kept pushing me forward. I also took up journaling. Writing down the madness helped me release the utter frustration and feelings of needing to give up. I needed this release so I could face the next round in the ring. Continuing to play the game was tiring, and I'd take breaks for a few days to collect my hurt feelings, then I'd silently put them away in the proverbial box, never to be opened again. I felt like a Transformer toy clicking my armor on and morphing from a vehicle to a fighting machine. I needed to keep fighting if I wanted to win the prize.

Who was this woman I had turned into despite all my rules? I tried to draw some lessons from learning how to hold back my excitement before there was long-term evidence that a guy was there to stay. This rule of holding back was difficult, and I tried to find the balance between feeling a "little" hopeful after a good date, but not "too hopeful" that I would feel crushed if it didn't go well.

My advice to you, as you work on holding back, is to allow your support system to help remind you to stay in the day. Staying in the day and working on just being delighted during the date is key. Learning that "all we have is this date, and I'm going to stay in it and have a good time," without wondering if there will be another is the skill to hone. Try not to allow this finely crafted skill to turn into a fear of waiting for the other shoe to drop. Sometimes, I would swing too far the other way, thinking that every time things felt good, something bad was bound to happen. This created extreme anxiety that could be difficult to manage. I told myself that if I started to jump to "gloom and doom" instead of staying in the moment, and perhaps even being cautiously optimistic, I would have to take a break. But I remained determined, so I continued to plunge through the ups and downs of the roller coaster ride, holding my clutch in place but remaining hopeful I could let them hatch one day. I knew that if I was still willing to do this, I needed to pull up my big girl pants and carry on. So I did. And you can too.

One monkey off your back,
but the circus is still in town.

CHAPTER 8

There's Always
Another One

I've mentioned my support team more than once: friends who helped me, collectively and individually through many years of distance running and the past few years we called the "broken years."

Christie is a married mother of five children ages eleven to twenty-one. She is no nonsense and has always been the calm to my storm. Like most of us, Christie has her stressors, but you wouldn't know it if you weren't in her inner circle as she always exudes calmness and coolness. My intense personality, coupled with all the things in my life that shifted on the day I broke my leg, needed her even-keeled nature in many ways. After my divorce, she would pop over to my house to help put together new bedroom furniture, provide moral support when my kids were acting out, and lend a balanced and rational ear to my high level of anxiety. With all the time she was spending with me, we joked that she had become my COVID wife. I'm not sure if she realized how powerful that statement was, or if she even knows the magnitude of my gratitude to her that continues to grow with every moment we spend together. In my circle of pals, she's the problem solver who lends good advice, empathizes with the crazy, and always reassured me that "there's always another one."

This became another one of my mantras that carried me through some dark days. *Christie says there's always another one*, I would tell myself, over and over. The facts pointed to an endless supply of guys; it just got hard to continue sharing my story and investing my energy, even if minimally, just to have the guys disappear. But chuckling with Christie and my running friends, shaking our heads together, and remembering that there was always another one, allowed for a light in the darkness during a time that felt so hopelessly crazy.

So we ran, and talked, and walked, and talked, and hiked, and talked, and processed, and moved forward. As the men came and went, the therapeutic conversations with my friends got me to a place where I was ready to persevere. The power of women and distance running is undeniable. Our problems were never fixed per se, but as we talked and dumped and offered thoughts on each of our life journeys, we felt fixed enough to get back in our cars and face our days. We'd lovingly call out, "Talk to you in five minutes," as we knew we'd be group messaging throughout the morning, afternoon, and night, lending an ear to whomever needed it. And with a bunch of women whose mornings started sometimes earlier than 5:00 a.m., there was quite a bit of material to work through. This process of being vulnerable and open with other women as we exerted our bodies cleared our souls so we could function in a world that could be relentless. As you read all these stories and wonder how I continued to ride the circus rides, know that this chapter is dedicated to the folks on the ride with me, strapped in virtually by my side. It was the only way to date online.

When I think about there always being another one, I feel a bit guilty that I resorted to thinking of men like a delicious glass of wine or a bag of my favorite sour gummy candy: *No need to fret; you can always go back for another flavor if what you have isn't the one for you.* As men would come and go, it felt like I had to think of them like this to minimize the devastation that came from failed encounters.

I met Phil during the height of the pandemic. He was in his midforties, had never been married, had no kids, and had a great job in medical sales. It's funny that I haven't spoken about him until now, as he was one to remember in some ways but simply forgettable in others. He was extremely kind, communicative, responsive, loved his family, had friends, took care of his home, and loved to cook. He made me laugh and wanted to learn about who I was.

When Phil matched with me on the app, I had just blocked another guy who had been incredibly dirty on our very first exchange, asking me if I would come over to his house to "sit on his face." I told Phil what had happened just before we connected. He noted he wasn't surprised, and came across like an empathetic, fun gentleman. We laughed about the smutty comments people often made in the beginning of an app conversation and commiserated while comparing stories. It was a refreshing change in the circus act to something a little smoother and more comfortable, like the folks on acrobat rings, gliding and flowing through their number without incident and with such ease. Even if it was a big no-no for a first date, I agreed to meet Phil at his house. It was at the height of the pandemic, and bars and restaurants were closed due to the health risks. I told my friends where I'd be, got pretty, and drove twenty minutes to meet this nice-enough dude.

We ended up dating for a month or so, but in the end, the intimacy wasn't working like it needed to. It was so disappointing because he checked so many boxes, but that unchecked one was important and proved to be the deal breaker.

Phil was healing from past relationship issues that affected him when he was connecting intimately with me. When it came to intimacy, he was very timid and vanilla, a passive style that didn't match my spark. Any time our kissing led to the bedroom, he got shy, uncomfortable, and awkward. He was desperately afraid to touch my nipples in any way, as he felt that would be too rough. Frankly, this surprised me, since two of my best features sit pretty high and large on my chest, and look damn good for a woman of my age. I've been known to turn ass-men into breast-men overnight, so this threw me for a loop. Don't get me wrong. I'm not a super kinky girl, but this guy was so timid, it wasn't attractive. Having someone avoid that area seemed sad, wrong, and a bit strange. He shared that in his past relationship, his girlfriend demanded some rough and kinky stuff in the bedroom, which made him hesitate now, in even the smallest ways, to be assertive. This lack of good sexual chemistry hurt our progress, and we both agreed we were not a match in this area. Phil was boring in the bedroom, and, while having someone who was serious about meeting a life partner was different and refreshing, I needed more than what he had to offer. Sigh—there's always another one.

Max the Drummer was another younger man, but he was interested in meeting someone older, and our mutual love of heavy metal music bonded us immediately. We texted for a few weeks before he came over. The weeks of texting had given me a sense of comfort, and I admit I bent my rule of meeting in a public place first. Nothing bad happened, but I would advise to be careful of breaking this rule. But he ended up being a guy who was much braver over the phone than in person.

We sat on the couch, watching a movie, and, frankly, he seemed terrified of me. He was afraid to hold my hand, had a very stiff posture, wouldn't look me in the eye, and seemed to hesitate with his words. This hadn't been the case when we communicated by text. When he left that night, we agreed to another date, despite things feeling awkward, but it never happened. Later, I heard from him randomly. And I suppose his interest in me was high, but his bravery for meeting in person was low.

Many months later, he asked me for a picture of my feet. Turns out he had a foot fetish and that had been his real reason for connecting with me. *Oh, Max, are you serious? A picture of my feet?* I'm embarrassed to admit I gave this some serious consideration. Feet are harmless right? And, despite a long-distance running career, my feet are probably an eight out of ten on the sexy, cute-toes scale. But did I want him to think this was something I was willing to engage in regularly? I decided that pictures of body parts couldn't lead to anything mature and healthy, so I moved on and remembered: *There's always another one.*

It was like being on a treasure hunt without a map, and I couldn't even pinpoint what I was looking for. But I was discovering what I didn't want: someone who was dirty right off the bat, timid, aggressive, inconsiderate, wouldn't text back, egotistical, unhealthy, trauma filled, selfish, dishonest, racist, or unchivalrous. But what I was hoping to find? I hoped that when I found it, I'd know, and then I'd be able to describe it. So I pressed on, tapping into my adventurous spirit and searching blindly in a maze of confusion.

Tyler the EMT and Ethan the Super Young were in the queue for quite some time, but didn't move past communicating with their thumbs or being an occasional voice on the other end of the line.

Tyler was surprised when our phone conversation lasted over an hour. Apparently, it was rare for him to feel such a strong connection just over the phone. I didn't tell him I always had good phone calls. I had a huge weeding-out process from the dating app to the first text, then from texting to the first phone call. The rules demanded this, and by the time a guy heard my voice, I was relatively sure it would go well. I decided I wouldn't hurt Tyler's feelings by telling him I was a therapist and could easily talk to a rock for hours. *Let the poor guy think he's special.* He said he would drive to see me after the side effects from his COVID shot wore off, but the next day he discovered that he had a severe case of COVID, made worse by getting the shot when he unknowingly had it. He texted me for few of days, complaining about how he felt and saying how badly he wanted to meet me. Then . . . he was gone.

Ethan was in his early twenties, and when he reached out to me, he commented about my job instead of my looks in my profile picture. That intrigued me. Although he never ghosted me, texting with him was like being in a game of tug of war: leaning into the idea of meeting me, then leaning away without connecting. I knew this one wasn't going to work, but it was a slow week at the circus, so I figured, why not let him talk me into a date? Even after a long phone call, his fear of meeting me in person persisted. We made a date, which he found an excuse to cancel. Any other plans never solidified into a true day and time. So many of these guys appeared so brave at first, when they were texting and talking on the phone, only to pull back when the idea of meeting me became imminent. They were becoming part of a club, so to speak. The ones who talk bravely and act weakly. Ethan joined the fear club, as his bravery only survived outside of the real, and this became a game left for the young ones, as this old cougar was just plain over it.

When I would get discouraged, I'd remember to not

"count my chickens," and that "there is always another one." This self-talk would help dispel the all-or-nothing thinking that crept into my brain when I continued to be disappointed.

My friend Stacey and I would talk about whether we were beginning to hate all men. Obviously, I didn't hate them, but it was something I said often: "What an asshole. I hate men." All my married friends, most of them with sons, agreed. I mean, the guys' track records those many months had been horrific. Did it make me feel better to say they were all the same and give up trusting them? Sometimes it did—when I said it in jest, in anger, or frustration. But of course I didn't hate them. If I did, I wouldn't have continued to try to find "the one."

But I hated their behavior. I wondered if I would ever find one who was able to take care of himself, who could and wanted to communicate, who respected me and would love me for who I was. Would I find someone who didn't *need* me but *wanted* me?

Of course bad behavior isn't gender specific. Some of these men were coming from relationships with women who had treated them awfully. So, while I'd love to play the blame game, unhealthy jumps gender lines. I guess I must realize that, and as I say to myself that there is always another one, I have to also believe that the next one could be the one. We only need one, right?

So the treasure hunt continued. With my self-talk intact, my friends in the ring with me, and the circus in full swing, I kept looking for another one, believing that one day the game would end, and the hunt would reveal the prize.

Peep show, anyone?

CHAPTER 9

My Dick Circus Is Vast

Peep shows have been a part of our history for over a century, allowing folks to look through a viewing slot, or a hole, to see a live sex show. During the rise of the pornographic industry in the 1970s, they became even more popular, until the internet introduced an even more expansive opportunity to "show your stuff," especially in the online dating world.

Old circuses sometimes featured peep shows, but the person viewing the action usually did so by choice; they paid, they peeked, they were entertained, and they left. But in the online dating peep show, there's a different idea about consent: The myth of the unsolicited dick pic is true. You may have thought that this was folklore, something so sensational, there's no way it could be truth. Someone clearly speaks about such things to get a laugh and be funny, but there is *no way* a stranger would text a pic of his dick—let alone a *video* of wetting his hand and stroking his cock, just to show me "what I would be getting." Right? No way? Yes way!

The guy who sent the video stooped even lower and texted that if I met him at a hotel (no time for dinner, only sex) and serviced us both, I wouldn't be sorry.

> I am offering if you want to stop by for an hour or two for a few rounds with this big dick. Would love to please you however ya' want. That's what turns me on the most. The other feels as good as they can.

I told him he wasn't looking for a date, but a prostitute, and he said, "Oh, I'd never stoop that low." *What!?* Pretty sure the stoop is in the upright position, and you're perched on it high and tight like a shiny pelican. Yep, you're stooping buddy. You may as well own your shit!

Alas, men truly believe that, because *they* are visual creatures and need to see our bodies to decide our worth, we want to see theirs. It doesn't matter how big or small it is, but it's always hard, and their hand is always pushing down hard to create a lengthening effect. There is always something shiny on it, and it always seems to be zoomed in. (Since I have large-screen phone for my old lady eyes, I got to see these big surprises on an extra-large scale, sometimes with a label in the large bold font of my phone setting.) I get it. It's nice and big and happy. But really? Come on!

Do some women want to see these pics? Before even

starting a conversation? Maybe—and if so, I'm not judging. But not many adult women looking for love want to see the goods on the front end of the story. Women are mostly emotional beings. We want a real connection, and if we decide we want to see you naked, in person is the way we roll. And no, you can't have a picture of my body. I mean, why? I'm a respectable, professional woman. Sure I like sex—and everything that goes with it. But when I send something to your phone, it's now yours to share, so I choose what I send wisely. Conversely, don't think your dick wasn't shared with all my friends. We laughed and thought you were ridiculous, and it immediately made me want to block you and the horse you rode in on.

For men, the moral of this little story is: *Ask!* "Can I send you an amazing, hot, sexy, large picture of my man parts?" Communication is key, boys, and when you think your penis speaks louder than your words, you're just dead wrong. And by the way, it's just not that pretty. Or big. Really it's not.

I was always astonished at how quickly and easily a dick would arrive on my phone. How did a guy assume it was a good idea to put the cart before the horse—the pic before the actual dick? As I studied the sample size of men who did this—and remember I probably talked to at least 200, with over 100 moving over to texting from the messaging in the app—it looked like it was a thing with young dudes. When we texted on the app, they couldn't send a pic, so that sample size wouldn't be accurate. I often would give them my phone number quickly, just to test my theories and see whether or not they would "go there" too soon. I gave my number to about 100 of them—the guys you saw in the intermission—and waited to see what would happen. Often, the younger guys would send a picture faster than I could text them one word. They were Millennials and Gen Zs in their twenties and thirties who all grew up in the information age. I wondered if sending dick pics and talking dirty immediately was a norm for this age group? I'm not a prude, but I didn't understanding being plunged into the world of "see it on screen before you see it in person." I wanted to be eased into things.

As time went on, when guys sent me their dick pics, my reply texts would vary depending on my mood. If I needed some material for my run with my girls the next morning, I would engage them with variations of "Wow, that was fast!" or "What made you think I wanted to see you so soon?" If my intuition was screaming that the guy needed to go, I would block him. Sometimes, the dick pics and creepy stories would merge into one interaction. After he sent his dick pic, one guy texted about taking me into his sadomasochistic dungeon. That guy got blocked before I could even blink!

The very first dick pic I got in the circus was Monte the Golf Pro's. This was about three weeks into my foray with the dating app. Monte was in his early thirties, and our chat had started off normally enough with typical questions like: "What are you looking for?" and "Do you want to meet up?" But right after I told him I wanted to talk on the phone before we met in person, he sent me a picture of a hard, large penis, his hand gripping its base and pulling down forcefully to create an illusion of a larger shaft. It was shiny and curved toward his belly. I wondered if it was a live picture, or if he had staged it long ago for his standard first pic send-off. Monte said it was his, and that this is what I had to look forward to.

I told him if I hadn't asked for it, I didn't want it. But I pride myself on having a good sense of humor, so instead of blocking him immediately, I entertained myself by engaging with him on what I had coined "COVID dirty texting." Since the health pandemic was raging, it was difficult to know where to meet someone if you decided they were worth the risk. He texted that he wanted to go for a hike and then have sex in the woods. And as my mouth hung open, I texted back:

> You can't take me to dinner because of COVID, but you want to know where we are going to fuck in the woods? Won't we get "close" when we do that? At the very least, feed me first!

I wondered if his behavior was actually common, and I'd just been out of the loop for too long. Or had this seemingly nice guy gone totally rogue after being inside for weeks without human contact? Was this behavior a sign I should move on? It was hard to know in the beginning. But I decided to go with my gut and move along, because I needed to observe these animals in this new habitat a little longer. This dude was a golf pro at a country club close to my house, so his dick wasn't even totally anonymous. I could probably go over there right now, ask for him, cock my head, smile, and say, "Remember me? Or am I one of the many women who have seen the goods before the guy?"

I learned to state up front that I didn't want to see pictures like these, making sure to mention that I am an in-person girl who wants an emotional connection before beginning a physical one. This weeded out many of the overtly sexual freaks, but Dave the Beer Guy (he worked for a beer distributor) slipped through the cracks.

In his midthirties, Dave was what I like to call a slow creeper. We texted for a few days, and he was appropriate and fun in a flirty way. He complimented me, staying right on the edge of smutty: he would call me sexy in one sentence, and in the next tell me that my job as a therapist sounded interesting and rewarding. He texted that his sex life was "non-existent lately" and how hard that was for him and his sex drive, only to stop there and mention how important it was for him to have an emotional connection before an intimate one. I was lured in with the idea of balance and that, while this guy seemed a little dirty, he also had good qualities such as wanting a real connection. But then it came, and it wasn't the typical naked dick. Oh no. It was a hard one shrouded by a blanket because Dave the Beer Guy didn't want to insult me by sending me the real thing—but he did want to warn me about its size. Apparently, his last girlfriend couldn't handle it, and he wanted to make sure I was up for the challenge. He was doing me a "service" by letting me know how important it was to him that I could handle such a large package and not be "scared off." What was I supposed to say to that? "Don't worry. I've had two children, so my vagina should be just fine." Or, "Oh baby, I love them nice and large, and I can't wait to fit that thing inside of me." Maybe he wanted my reaction to be fear—after all, some guys like that. I believe my response was, "I'm sure I'll be just fine, Dave."

He must have thought that was an invitation to go bigger and bolder, because out came the naked dick—and, boy, was it big. I must have been going through a dating dry spell at the time, because I actually considered meeting him despite the pictures. But after two weeks of texting, calling, pictures, and flirting, he ghosted me. Why had he bothered to put in all that time and emotional energy just to vanish? It made me wonder if some guys were on the dating app only for the texting entertainment. Maybe it was for an orgasmic thrill? Send a picture, masturbate, play some games, then leave? Shock with their cocks and then go.

———

When my friend Carolyn and I went away for a girls' weekend in a cabin in the woods, she asked me how fast I could get a dick on my phone. Carolyn's married with three kids, hasn't dated or flirted in over two decades, and was clueless about this new dating world, even if, as a therapist who works with young women, she'd heard about dick pics. She asked, "Do they really send them to you without your asking?"

"Oh yeah," I said. "I bet I can get one in under ten minutes."

Our inner, giggly teenage girls had come out, and I admit I took the challenge. I went to the dating site and clicked "Like" on a gorgeous, young aspiring country music singer named Tyler. He responded immediately. Since the dating app I used didn't have a "send pictures" feature, I sent him my phone number. Without any preamble, he texted he'd be in my area for work the following week and would love to meet me at a hotel for a quickie.

Then it happened. And it wasn't just a dick pic, but a video of him spitting on his hand, then stroking his penis—eight minutes after I had clicked "Like"! I screamed to Carolyn, "Here you go girl, a porn clip for your viewing pleasure." She hopped over to my side of the couch, and we laughed hysterically, gazing upon what we had received. I can't say I'm proud of this, but all's fair in love and war, and if a guy's willing to send it, that's on him—and his big dick.

I knew I was playing the same game the guys were, and I worked at rationalizing that, telling myself that a little dirty game play wasn't a big deal. It was difficult to always remain serious in the dating search. Just like at the circus, you can be lured in ways you didn't expect. I found myself swinging between two types of men: the ones who could possibly turn into something real, and the ones who would just be an entertaining story, a part of the game.

But as I lay in bed at night, evaluating what I was doing, I knew deep down I had to decide whether I was still looking for something casual but monogamous, or was I ready to get serious? At this point, I'd been dating for almost two years. And for some people, that's not a long time—my sister's been dating for two decades. One of her friends had dated for six months and thought she'd finally found Mr. Right. It was quick to get serious, and she asked him repeatedly if what they had was the real thing. And after flowers, fancy dinners, and constant reassurance that he was all in, he dumped her without an explanation, saying only that he would have to live with how he hurt her. It made me think that maybe I should just throw in the online dating towel and stop putting my money in the machine, hoping for some shiny prize in return. But that wasn't my style. I was a fighter, and I was determined.

It *was* time to get serious. My time in the peep show tent was over, and while it had provided laughs, it wasn't what I wanted or needed in the long term. I wanted to find my guy, and it wouldn't be one whose dick I saw before I saw his face. Maybe my guy would be more old-fashioned than I knew existed, but often we receive what we need, and not what we thought we wanted. I was ready to see what someone with integrity had to offer, and the idea of someone holding back until the right time seemed perfect to me. I said good-bye to casual.

———

While these experiences were teaching me to know what to say and how to say it, how to interpret, and how to navigate, I'll admit to playing around and being vague sometimes. There was a part of me that wanted to see how far guys would push the limits, which also revealed a lot about their basic character. I decided that a little bit of engaging allowed me to test how quickly they would become gross. Perhaps this wasn't fair and bordered on playing games with them. After all, I was looking for an honest and genuine guy to date, but I engaged in the circus acts as well. The message here is that there will be days you feel like playing around, and days that you go back to your original hunt. The hunting gets tiring, so playing around lightens the mood—but trusting your gut is imperative. (Be sure to have a lesson in how to block someone if you are technologically challenged. This tool should definitely be in your toolbox.)

Decide on any given day what you feel you can do and engage at will. Just know who you are, and what your goal should be.

It's the greatest show on Earth!
Stay for a while.

CHAPTER 10

Is It Worth It?

Despite the ups and downs, the creepy and the crude, the twenty months I spent in the online dude circus were worth it. My journey eventually led me to someone special. When I think about the meaning of the journey, it reminds me of my love-hate relationship with distance running.

In distance running, there are good runs, bad runs, stressful runs, angry runs, runs where you laugh the whole time, and runs that you never want to do again. My friends and I run to finish races not to win—victory isn't the ultimate goal. Keeping our eyes on the goal gives us motivation to endure the harder parts of the journey, and the meaning is in the training. We learn what shoes work best, what brand of socks our feet like, and what bra will chafe your cleavage within minutes. We learn what to do differently next time, what our favorite distance is, and we find that the mental health release comes during the training. Similarly, the online dating journey taught me how to have resilience, determination, hope, humor, resolve, and grit. I learned the need to ask for support more than I ever had in the past, and I learned that what I thought I wanted in the beginning was not what I needed in the end.

You will need to decide for yourself if you want to buy tickets to this dating circus and how many of the different acts you'll want to join. Your gut and heart will be your guides in the almost daily decision to stay for a while or take a break. You'll make the decision based on your resilience and your tolerance for being a glutton for punishment while you wait out the freak-show tent. The time you spend at this circus can change who you are as a person, and not always in positive ways.

As I mentioned earlier, I attributed the feelings that affected my self-evaluation during this time to a type of traumatic experience. So much like the trauma we work with in a therapy setting, these feelings enter our brains in insidious ways and emerge when we least expect them. Of course online dating trauma isn't a real diagnosis, but perhaps it should be. Depending on the baseline personality and health of an individual, it can come in different forms: it made me doubt my intuition, worry about lack of constant communication and contact, and created a layer of self-doubt I had never experienced before. Even with my broken leg and broken marriage, I still felt supported by a lot of people, and my self-esteem remained intact. It wasn't until I entered the circus of ghosts and zombies that I started to doubt myself. Even with all the laughs and girl talks, in the quiet moments, alone in my bed at night, I began to take it all personally.

I have a great life, full of wonderful people who build me up, so how could I let some men on the other end of the phone tear me down? It's hard to figure out, even after being a therapist for almost three decades. Perhaps we all have our limits, and after almost two years of getting dumped by online mystery men, I started to feel my armor erode. The only solution was to build new armor, a shield around my heart. Just like the fighting Saxons and Danes in the 800s formed walls with their shields to repel the enemy's sword and arrow attacks, I formed one around my heart as tightly as I could. This way, I could keep entering the circus's battle ring yet keep my heart intact when the man in the ring with me disappeared into the shadows after a plunging blow.

A man ghosts me after three days? I just push on with my fresh sword and shield. A man doesn't text back when he says he will? I gather my army of women and guard myself. But despite my medieval resolve, these things still hurt. This trauma started to affect me in a way that seeped into the back of the battlefield when my guards weren't watching. And it almost took me out.

But I stayed in the center ring, fighting for what I

continued to believe was worth it. I summoned up the most steadfast and fierce faith of those ninth-century warriors. The Saxons believed in one God and in heaven, and the Danes believed in many pagan gods and Valhalla. They all would die, fighting for what they believed in and knowing beyond a doubt that they were going someplace good. I, too, had faith in the idea that my person was out there, and I would continue to press the limits of my shell to find him. I'm not sure where the faith came from. It's hard to know the source of our hopes and dreams that turns into a belief that something good will happen.

Deciding if something is worth continuing despite it being difficult is a challenge I'd taken on before. I only took up distance running when I was thirty-eight. I don't have a traditional long and lean runner's body, and besides dancing and drill team in high school, I didn't have an athletic past. Since I don't have the natural skills, running takes a lot of effort for me: it hurts, it's hard, and it never gets any easier. But the reward after the run and the therapeutic value that comes from the friendships formed along the way, make it something I continue to go back to. The feeling of accomplishment, chemical release, emotional release, and physical fitness are worth the fight.

At some point, my running girls and I decided to up our

game and run ultra-marathons. We can now complete twelve-hour races. The effort and training this takes sounds crazy to so many, but it's what we do. Staying the course, despite the pain and difficulty level, felt right to me, and perhaps gave me some of the resolve I took into online dating. The aphorism "life is a marathon, not a sprint" can be equated to searching for your perfect partner, and the patience and endurance aspect is quite similar: the qualities it takes to stay in something when it's hard are the same. Maybe all the years of hard running prepared me for the no pain–no gain game of the dude circus. And as in distance running, if there is no risk, there is no reward.

One day, while my friends and I were hashing out my latest ghosting story, I started wondering if I needed to step away from the show. I had been working hard to keep my self-esteem intact, and I had used a lot of energy up with the constant "introduction texting." I was depleted and tired. But I decided to rally. I'm not totally clear about the reasons I decided to stay the course, but I think I was trying to prove that there had to be a male counterpart for me. My logical deduction was that, if I'm here, and I'm not crazy, then *all* guys can't be crazy or asshats. And while I admit I can succumb to emotion, I am rational when it comes to decision making. I also knew that my friends would miss the humor and excitement that came from my stories. When I sent my running girls excerpts from the chapters of this book as I was writing it, they'd laugh, saying they could hear me through the words and picture the story as it unfolded.

As I reflect now on every date, nickname in my contact list, hope, disappointment, shock, humorous moment, inconceivable behavior, and wild roller coaster ride, I wouldn't change a thing. Life has become about the experiences along the journey, as much as, or maybe even more than, it is about the prize at the end. And in my case, my diligence and persistence in staying at the circus paid off, as the ultimate prize of finding a partner happened. But every decision we make along this dating path serves a purpose. I learned that to be self-aware, to know who I am, and to find my own truth, the journey was an important part of the process.

It was worth it for me. Deciding whether it will be for you is a personal decision, but know that whether you choose to never to check out this type of dating or you decide that this circus of men is something you want to engage in, you can always change your mind—over and over again. You can hopscotch over the men who want friends with benefits and skip to the ones who want a wife. You can stand with one foot on a square that promises fun but not seriousness, and you can see what your balancing skills are while you're there.

You can turn in a circle with your feet apart and plant them down together on two men at a time if casual dating is for you. The beauty of your own personal learning curve is that you create your own zig-zagging path, going forward and backward and changing your mind as you decide how you want to play the game. And as you hone your skills, become part of the show, and find stable footing with your decisions, you will know in your heart and in your gut, whether to continue or not. You can buy your ticket to the circus and then head right out the back door, only to come back in when you're ready. The most important part is knowing you get to make the choice.

So, I decided to click on one more guy before I deleted the app. He started talking to me within a day, and although he seemed nice and we had some things in common, I couldn't have guessed what was about to happen to my own journey. I was about to leave the circus, and I didn't even know it. And when the time came, I was ready and excited. I can only believe that it was because of the time I spent in the circus that I knew this was my guy. If I had met Ben earlier, maybe it wouldn't have been the right time. My advice is to remember that there is value in all parts of your online dating path, and they all lead you to where you eventually need to be.

Even the most entertaining show
comes to an end.

CHAPTER 11

My Unicorn

R ight now I'm in the middle of what I'd love to call the last chapter. But how do we know when any relationship we begin is the last? Society tells us to search for our one true love: the one to grow with, build a home and family with, and get old with. But as many divorced people know, that's pretty unrealistic. Who was the first idiot who came up with the notion that we have one soul mate and that we need to gut it out until the end? What if the more realistic belief is that we change and grow toward different people, and that maybe we'll have a few soul mates in our lifetime? Someone who is meant to be at this current time in our lives. I've adopted a new saying: "This is for now, not forever." It helps me recognize that there are different reasons and seasons for different experiences.

When we're young, we want that one true love filled with romance. We go from high school boyfriends to college dating, and then by young adulthood, it's time to search for *the one guy*. Most of us fantasize about the man we will walk down the aisle toward. Perhaps we even thought about our dress, our hair, and where the party will be.

I wanted someone who was handsome, successful, confident, and fun. I didn't think about qualities that would make a good father or if someone wanted to cook for me. I didn't necessarily search for a partner. I didn't realize I needed to specifically look for someone who didn't have to be asked to be a parent and didn't have to be asked to empty the dishwasher. I was looking for romance and excitement. After decades of marriage and then divorce, I still found myself still looking for someone who was fun, handsome, and successful. But mostly, I wanted to find someone who was self-sufficient and selfless. Someone who'd take care of me just as much as I would take care of him. Someone who could fix things and know how to problem solve without always needing me. I also knew what I didn't want. Before-marriage dating, you're looking for love; after-divorce dating, you're looking to avoid insanity. I didn't want someone who talked about his money and possessions like I should worship him, and I didn't want someone who was so self-centered he didn't ask me about myself. This type of insanity isn't the kind that needs to be hospitalized in a psychiatric unit, but it's the type that causes years of sadness, distress, and despair when you attempt to connect with someone with these characteristics.

But insane is exactly what you get when you dive into the internet. When I kept trying the different apps, I was determined to see if there was the "male version of me" out there. If I was here, and I wasn't crazy, there *had* to be a guy like that too, right? Isn't that why we go on these apps in the first place? To search in this new way to find our match? And then when we think we've found it . . . when do we trust it? Because the online dating culture teaches you to never expect anything, never to trust, and never to believe anything is real. Until you stumble upon real.

I was talking to one of my friends about my new guy and some of his incredible qualities, and she said, "Wow! You give me hope. You found a unicorn." When I think of a unicorn, I picture a beautiful mythical creature. It's white, with a gorgeous horn, and a mane that looks like a rainbow. It's not real of course, and like the circus, it's a creature of fantasy and excitement. Along with this gorgeous fantasy comes a definition: "Something that is highly desirable, but difficult to find or obtain." And my friend was right. I had found a unicorn, a diamond in the rough, a man unlike any I had ever met with the exception of my father.

Unlike a unicorn, Ben is real. I stumbled upon his picture

and profile one day during one of my typical scrolls. He had a long skinny beard, he camped, he climbed towers, and he had a cute pit bull. He was forty-five. So, I thought, *What the hell; I'm going to click like on his picture and see what happens.* I'd been at this for twenty months, and I was growing exhausted and weary of a process that felt like another job. I held out little hope, but I took a little breath and wondered if he would answer back. And then—there he was. We exchanged the usual meet-and-greet interactions, and I quickly realized that he might be someone I wanted to get to know better.

Ben was kind, sweet, and communicated his thoughts. We had a strong connection in many ways. He made me laugh. He owned his own business and home but didn't wear his success in a way that was off-putting. He was vulnerable with me, being honest with wanting to go slowly, but also telling me he was feeling the type of feelings that meant this could be something special. His behavior matched his words. He could cook, and I mean really cook. He loved his daughters. He said that he often has a stoic face, but he showed me other faces: the quirky smile when I said something outrageous, the intense stare when we kissed for hours. And I mean hours. I felt this one in my belly. In my toes. In my heart. It was fast but it wasn't. At our age, didn't we know when something felt right?

When two people come together, bringing baggage from

their lives before the relationship, it's hard to know what you can—and should—expect. I decided that if the person can own whatever they did in the past to contribute to the demise of a relationship and knows what they need to do differently this time, I can handle quite a bit.

Ben is a relationship trauma survivor. He has been married twice, but his last marriage rocked his world. When he told me about it, I realized his ex was so intensely mentally ill, it taught him to trust carefully, keep his feelings inside, go slowly with someone new, and make sure that whoever she was, she'd be liberal in thinking and open-minded in her beliefs.

I chuckle now when I think about the rules he set during the first two weeks of our dating story. We were to go slowly in all ways: physically, emotionally, and mentally. But alas, he couldn't follow his own rules, and by date four, he was cooking for me at his house. When he asked, "Are you staying the night?" I laughed so hard and said, "I'd love to, but is that going slowly?"

"No, it's not," he replied.

"Okay," I said, "but if I stay, it means that this is real."

"Yes, it definitely means that."

I wanted to stay—badly—but I didn't have a toothbrush . . . or pajamas. Oh, boy! But we managed, and recently, I graduated to having my own drawer at his house. Crossing that line from dating to "really dating" has been wonderful, and gets less scary all the time. When he calls me his "girlfriend" around other people, it makes me feel like a giddy teenage girl. I have no idea why that label makes me feel the way it does, but "belonging" to him in this way makes me smile at how I've shifted my perspective on hope and expectations. Ben is my unicorn. He'd say we are unicorns together, as his modesty runs deep and his thoughts around his characteristics being "rare" in my experience with men surprises him. And while I'm not sure how he feels about my nickname for him, I hope he realizes how special it means he is.

It's been hard to trust a new relationship. I keep telling Ben it's not him, but the endless days, weeks, and months of being let down. In the beginning, I probably asked too often if we were okay or if I'd said something that bothered him. I was so used to things changing on a dime and was tired of laughing about it. I told him I was a huge weirdo when it came to texting back, meaning: please text me back in a reasonable time or I will worry you are gone or dead. Over time, those feelings have abated, but I had to work hard not to fall into negative thinking patterns I'd become accustomed to.

Real feelings were developing, and I was afraid I was getting too emotionally invested. One day I asked him, "Can I let myself feel everything I'm feeling? Can I allow myself to fall down the rabbit hole of emotion?" Ben shows his love in actions not words, so when he told me, "Yes, you can fall," I allowed myself to trust and fall. Remember the game kids play, when you have to blindly fall backward, hoping someone will catch you? Letting yourself go, because you knew the person behind you earned the implicit trust that you felt? With Ben, I felt it more than I've ever felt it before in my life, so I fell hard. I'm totally and completely in love with a man I met on the same app that influenced me to write a book about the need to make the insanity comedic. Crazy, right?

In the middle of falling for Ben and feeling all the emotions I had hoped to find with someone new, his father was diagnosed with late-stage lung cancer. This has allowed us both to navigate deeper into each other. I've been able to show Ben who I am through this. How I'm a listener and a helper. How I'm not a judger. How I'm strong and not afraid of his fear, sadness, pain, and despair.

He keeps a lot of bolder emotions close to the vest, and while he is a high-level communicator about what he is thinking and doing, communicating feelings is a bit tougher for him. Life on life's terms hit us at only two months in, and so far, we are navigating it with everything we have.

Allowing someone to be who they are when you know that if you push a little, they could feel even more supported than they already do, is a balancing act—one I'm truly willing to do, every single day.

And as I've exited the online dating circus, I'm still reminded of this theme: Picture the circus performer high up in the air on that tight rope. They can't move too much one way or the other, or disaster strikes. This is how I'm operating. I will be supportive but let him come to me when he wants to talk. I will offer help and accept when he might not want it. I will cancel our weekend away without a thought because family comes first, but I will also tease that he owes me one, since humor has its place in many things. I will gently push sometimes, and back off most of the time—not my strong suit, but I'm learning and growing and deciding that this man is certainly worth the effort it takes to hold that heavy balancing pole as we navigate across the tight rope together.

I've warned him about me. Told him I like to be in control. That I run my wild show at home and at my many jobs. But that I will always acquiesce when someone knows more than I do or when I'm not the expert. I will let someone else lead if I trust them. He seems to like these qualities.

I've begun to think that relationships have a bigger chance of working when there is no combined income, no small children to raise, and no shared household. Just meaningful and incredible time spent together—at least at first. Just last night, Ben told me that I was such a catch, so I'm starting to believe that perhaps I, too, have some qualities of a unicorn.

And so it begins: the hope that this will be the last chapter in my dating story. Is it possible that it took only twenty months? Maybe. Hopefully. Maybe this bizarre and winding road of dating taught me enough about myself and about the world of online men that I finally know that this is my person. And even if this doesn't work in the long term, I will try to take a page from the COVID times and work on living in the day, the hour, the moment, and remember that in life, if there is no risk, there's no reward. I know that Ben is definitely my "for now" guy, and perhaps even my "forever" guy. But we can't know, can we? Circus acts come in many forms, and while some are scary and backward and wrong, many are fun and exciting and worth it. And now that I'm more seasoned in this century's relationship circus, I feel like I can make you laugh and give you advice. So here it is.

Despite it all, I wouldn't change a thing. The new rules, the new language, the broken men, the dick pics, the lying, the craziness, the ongoing disappointment—it was all worth it. So there it is. Risk high, reach far, stay in it, don't settle, and stay the course. Because if your soul can take it, you will win big and laugh a lot along the way.

About the Author

I'm a fifty-year-old divorced therapist from the Midwest who has always been a writer but never an author—until now. I help people for a living, so naturally it made sense to write my first book about a topic that pushed at my own confidence and self-esteem.

I grew up in a loving family, the oldest sister, with a mom who stayed home with us and a dad who worked but always helped my mom, parented, and never needed to be asked to be involved in his kids' lives. Their marriage was the best role model of how relationships should look and feel. My parents are still married after nearly fifty-five years, so my role models are fiercely intact and lovingly supportive.

I went to college, got my master's in social work in the mid-1990s, and got married in the late 90s to someone I met at work. Twenty-two years later, I found myself broken and divorced while the world also seemed to be breaking, and this is when I decided dating would be a good idea. Little did I know what was waiting for me.

I am a "old lady distance runner" who started running

at age thirty-eight and never wanted to be competitive. I run to spend intentional time with some of my best friends, and it was on these runs that I would tell my dating stories. I got feedback, support, love, and most of all, a lot of laughter. "Rose, you have to write a book about these men." So, I did. I had to write about what was happening to be able to laugh and heal, and I realized, as my friends kept laughing, that humor was my coping mechanism.